To Be a Mother

To Be a Mother

compiled by

Wendi Momen

GEORGE RONALD • OXFORD
GEORGE RONALD, Publisher

46 High Street, Kidlington, Oxford OX5 2DN

© Wendi Momen 1997
All Rights Reserved

A Cataloguing-in Publication entry
is available from the British Library

ISBN 0-85398-421-2

Typeset by Leith Editorial Services, Abingdon, UK
Printed and bound in Great Britain by
Cromwell Press, Melksham, Wiltshire

Contents

To four generations of Bahá'í
mothers and daughters

Petrine Gunderson
Ann Gunderson Morris
Carol Cunningham Morris Allen
Carmel Cunningham Momen

Preface

'The great importance', the Universal House of Justice wrote in 1984, 'attached to the mother's role derives from the fact that she is the first educator of the child.'

Her attitude, her prayers, even what she eats and her physical condition have a great influence on the child when it is still in the womb. When the child is born, it is she who has been endowed by God with the milk which is the first food designed for it, and it is intended that, if possible, she should be with the baby to train and nurture it in its earliest days and months. This does not mean that the father does not also love, pray for, and care for his baby, but as he has the primary responsibility of providing for the family, his time to be with his child is usually limited, while the mother is usually closely associated with the baby during this intensely formative time when it is growing and developing faster than it ever will again

during the whole of its life. As the child grows
older and more independent, the relative
nature of its relationship with its mother and
father modifies and the father can play a
greater role.[1]

However:

Reverence for, and protection of, motherhood
have often been used as justification for
keeping women socially and economically
disadvantaged. It is this discriminatory and
injurious result that must change. Great
honour and nobility are rightly conferred on
the station of motherhood and the importance
of training children . . . The great challenge
facing society is to make social and economic
provisions for the full and equal participation
of women in all aspects of life while
simultaneously reinforcing the critical
functions of motherhood.[2]

It is in the spirit of both revering motherhood and
valuing the contribution women can make to the
wider community that this little book of verses
from the holy scriptures, poets and thinkers is
offered.

Acknowledgements

My heartfelt thanks to my friends Judith Brooke, Tony Mooney and Susan Simerley for their invaluable assistance and support, particularly during the period this book was being completed.

The publisher would like to thank the following for permission to reprint their copyrighted works.

Adrinka Press, Napa, CA, for Dorothy Hansen, 'My Texas Mother's Photograph'.

Houghton Mifflin Company for Anne Hempstead Branch, 'Her Hands'.

The National Spiritual Assembly of the Bahá'ís of the United States for material from *Two Wings of a Bird: The Equality of Women and Men*.

Natureagraph, Happy Camp, CA for Roger White, 'Mother'.

New Leaf Publishing, Richmond, B.C. for Roger White, 'Mother's Day'.

Random House UK Ltd and Simon and Schuster, New York, for quotations from M. Scott Peck, *The Road Less Travelled*.

On the Birth of a Child

Love is the very cause of life . . .
'Abdu'l-Bahá[1]

It is He Who created you from a single person,
and made his mate of like nature, in order that he
might dwell with her, in love. When they are
united, she bears a light burden and carries it
about, unnoticed. When she grows heavy, they
both pray to God their Lord, saying: 'If Thou
givest us a goodly child, we vow we shall (ever) be
grateful.'

Qur'án[2]

A human being is a single being.
Unique and unrepeatable.
John Paul II

I was not aware of the moment when I first
crossed the threshold of this life. What was the
power that made me open out into this vast
mystery like a bud in the forest at midnight!
When in the morning I looked upon the light I felt
in a moment that I was no stranger in this world,
that the inscrutable without name and form had
taken me in its arms in the form of my own
mother.

Rabindranath Tagore

Our birth is but a sleep and a forgetting;
The soul that rises with us,
     our life's star,
Hath had elsewhere its setting,
And cometh from afar:
Not in entire forgetfulness,
And not in utter nakedness,
But trailing clouds of glory do we come
From God, who is our home.

William Wordsworth

Little one, little one of my heart, I am thy first
love and the first to give thee a heart in love.

When I come near, thou smilest and stretchest
out thy little hands. And when I lift thee to me,
thou foldest thine arms about my neck, and
pressest thy smooth cheek to mine, calling me
love names in thy baby-talk.

What is there so sweet as love! and what is so
sweet as love at its dawning, new love, first love!

Yet night by night I kneel, and beg of Him
Who answers every prayer that through the
coming years He will make ever more deep and
sweet this early love of ours.

George Townshend[3]

We are thy teachers because God has appointed
us. You are to hear us because God wishes you to

do so. He made us your father and mother, because He chose that you should be taught by us.

We provide you with food and clothing and warmth. This is good; but the good of it will not last forever. The truth we teach you is the greatest of all the gifts we have to give you. Nothing else is important compared with this. Truth and the effects of truth last forever: not only for a little time. The teaching which God has told us to give you will make you more happy than clothes or houses or pleasure or money. People cannot be happy without truth, even on this earth: in the next world we shall be very unhappy without it.

Remember, these teachings are of more value than all else we have to give you. We teach you because we wish to obey God. We teach you not only because we love you very much, but for God's sake.

To teach you as God would have taught you is not easy. We are not so wise or so good as we should like to be; nor even so wise and good as we hope soon to become. God himself alone is a perfect teacher. We pray God constantly to help us; and because we so truly wish and strive to please Him He strengthens us with the power and wisdom of His Spirit. Whatever is true in our teaching, and whatever is good and right in it comes not from us, but from God.

George Townshend[4]

The Importance of Mothers

A man came to Prophet Muḥammad (peace be upon him) asking: 'O messenger of God! Who among the people is the most worthy of my good company?' The Prophet said, 'Your mother.' The man said, 'Then who else?' The Prophet said, 'Your mother.' The man asked again, 'Who else?' The Prophet said, 'Your mother.' The man continued to ask, 'Then who else?' Only then did the Prophet say, 'Your father.'

Reported by Al-Bukhari

It is clear . . . that the future generation depends on the mothers of today. Is not this a vital responsibility for the woman? Does she not require every possible advantage to equip her for such a task?

'Abdu'l-Bahá[1]

Women are the bearers of life-loving energy. Ours is the task of deepening that passion for life and separating from all that threatens life, all that diminishes life; becoming who we are as women; telling/living the truth of our lives; shifting the weight of the world.

Barbara Zanotti

It is undoubtedly the mother who plays the chief part in the life of a child. It is no exaggeration to say that the infant's power to receive suggestion from her is almost as great as his ability to draw milk from her breast. Put into other words, the baby reacts with unerring instinct to the mother's thoughts and feelings, even to the thoughts of which she is not fully conscious herself. The child has an astonishing ability to sense the atmosphere about him.

R. Edynbry[2]

The First Mentors

... mothers are the first educators, the first
mentors; and truly it is the mothers who
determine the happiness, the future greatness, the
courteous ways and learning and judgement, the
understanding and the faith of their little ones.

'Abdu'l-Bahá[1]

I have no answer for myself of thee,
Save that I learned beside my mother's knee;
'All is of God that is, and is to be;

And God is good.' Let this suffice us still,
Resting in childlike trust upon His will
Who moves to His great ends
        unthwarted by the ill.

John Greenleaf Whittier

The task of bringing up a Bahá'í child, as
emphasized time and again ... is the chief
responsibility of the mother, whose unique
privilege is indeed to create in her home such
conditions as would be most conducive to both
his material and spiritual welfare and
advancement. The training which a child first
receives through his mother constitutes the
strongest foundation for his future development,
and it should therefore be the paramount concern
of your wife ... to endeavour from now
imparting to her new-born son such spiritual

training as would enable him later on to fully
assume and adequately discharge all the
responsibilities and duties of Bahá'í life.

Shoghi Effendi[2]

The mother is the first teacher of the child. For
children, at the beginning of life, are fresh and
tender as a young twig, and can be trained in any
fashion you desire. If you rear the child to be
straight, he will grow straight, in perfect
symmetry. It is clear that the mother is the first
teacher and that it is she who establisheth the
character and conduct of the child.

Wherefore, O ye loving mothers, know ye that
in God's sight, the best of all ways to worship
Him is to educate the children and train them in
all the perfections of humankind; and no nobler
deed than this can be imagined.

'Abdu'l-Bahá[3]

O maid-servants of the Merciful! It is incumbent
upon you to train the children from their earliest
babyhood! It is incumbent upon you to beautify
their morals! It is incumbent upon you to attend
to them under all aspects and circumstances,
inasmuch as God – glorified and exalted is He! –
hath ordained mothers to be the primary trainers
of children and infants. This is a great and

important affair and a high and exalted position, and it is not allowable to slacken therein at all!

'Abdu'l-Bahá[4]

O handmaid of God! . . . To the mothers must be given the divine Teachings and effective counsel, and they must be encouraged and made eager to train their children, for the mother is the first educator of the child. It is she who must, at the very beginning, suckle the newborn at the breast of God's Faith and God's Law, that divine love may enter into him even with his mother's milk, and be with him till his final breath.

'Abdu'l-Bahá[5]

Darest thou
now, O soul
Walk out with me
towards the unknown region
Where neither ground is for the
feet, nor any path to follow?

Prepare thyself
for thou wilt have to
travel on alone.
The teacher can but point
the way. The path is one for

all, the means to reach the goal
must vary with the pilgrim.

Mme. Blavatsky

The Little Black Boy

. . . My mother taught me underneath a tree,
And, sitting down before the heat of day,
She took me on her lap and kissèd me,
And, pointing to the east, began to say:

'Look on the rising sun, – there God does live,
And gives us His light, and gives His heat away;
And flowers and trees and beasts and men receive
Comfort in morning, joy in noonday,
'And we are put on earth a little space,
That we may learn to bear the beams of love . . .'

William Blake

Children have more need of models than critics.

Carolyn Coats

Educating Mothers

. . . the education of women is of greater importance than the education of men, for they are the mothers of the race, and mothers rear the children. The first teachers of children are the mothers.

'Abdu'l-Bahá[1]

If it be considered through the eye of reality, the training and culture of daughters is more necessary than that of sons, for these girls will come to the station of motherhood and will mould the lives of the children. The first trainer of the child is the mother. The babe, like unto a green and tender branch, will grow according to the way it is trained. If the training be right, it will grow right, and if crooked, the growth likewise, and unto the end of life it will conduct itself accordingly.

Hence, it is firmly established that an untrained and uneducated daughter, on becoming a mother, will be the prime factor in the deprivation, ignorance, negligence and the lack of training of many children.

'Abdu'l-Bahá[2]

In former times it was considered wiser that woman should not know how to read or write; she should occupy herself only with drudgery. She was very ignorant. Bahá'u'lláh declares the

education of woman to be of more importance
than that of man. If the mother be ignorant, even
if the father have great knowledge, the child's
education will be at fault, for education begins
with the milk. A child at the breast is like a tender
branch that the gardener can train as he wills.

'Abdu'l-Bahá[3]

If, as she ought, the mother possesseth the
learning and accomplishments of humankind,
her children, like unto angels, will be fostered in
all excellence, in right conduct and beauty.

'Abdu'l-Bahá[4]

Women and girls must be educated – spiritually,
emotionally and intellectually – because a mother
cannot pass on what she does not have. A child
needs a nurturing environment and wise
guidance in the first years of life in order to
develop sound character and a well trained mind.
If the mother is unable, because of her own
deficiencies, to provide her children with
experiences which will equip them for later,
formal schooling, they will find themselves at a
serious, often crippling, disadvantage. It must be
stressed, however, that this dual responsibility of
developing the child's character and stimulating
his intellect also belongs to the family as a whole,

including the father and grandparents, and to the
community.

Bahá'í International Community[5]

Not only must girl children receive adequate
food, health care, and education, they must be
given every opportunity to develop their
capacities. As women become educated and enter
all fields of human endeavour, they will make
unique contributions to the creation of a just
world order – an order characterized by vigour,
cooperation, harmony, and a degree of
compassion never before witnessed in history. In
addition, as mothers they render an invaluable
service to humanity by educating the next
generation. In that capacity they will be the
primary agents for the transformation of society.
They, in particular, can inculcate in their children
the self-esteem and respect for others essential for
the advancement of civilization. It is clear, then,
that the station of mothers, increasingly
denigrated in many societies, is in reality of the
greatest importance and highest merit.

Bahá'í International Community[6]

The question of training the children and looking
after the orphans is extremely important, but
most important of all is the education of girl
children, for these girls will one day be mothers,

and the mother is the first teacher of the child. In whatever way she reareth the child, so will the child become, and the results of that first training will remain with the individual throughout his entire life, and it would be most difficult to alter them. And how can a mother, herself ignorant and untrained, educate her child? It is therefore clear that the education of girls is of far greater consequence than that of boys. This fact is extremely important, and the matter must be seen to with the greatest energy and dedication.

'Abdu'l-Bahá[7]

If the mother is educated
    then her children will be well taught.
When the mother is wise,
    then will the children be led into the path of
    wisdom.
If the mother be religious
    she will show her children how they should
    love God.
If the mother is moral
    she guides her little ones into the ways of
    uprightness.

'Abdu'l-Bahá[8]

. . . the education of woman is more necessary and important than that of man, for woman is the trainer of the child from its infancy. If she be

defective and imperfect herself, the child will
necessarily be deficient; therefore, imperfection
of woman implies a condition of imperfection in
all mankind, for it is the mother who rears,
nurtures and guides the growth of the child. This
is not the function of the father. If the educator
be incompetent, the educated will be
correspondingly lacking. This is evident and
incontrovertible. Could the student be brilliant
and accomplished if the teacher is illiterate and
ignorant? The mothers are the first educators of
mankind; if they be imperfect, alas for the
condition and future of the race.

'Abdu'l-Bahá[9]

Mothering

Her Hands

My mother's hands are cool and fair.
    They can do anything.
Delicate mercies hide them there
    Like flowers in the spring.

When I was small and could not sleep,
    She used to come to me,
And with my cheek upon her hand
    How sure my rest would be.

For everything she ever touched
    Of beautiful or fine,
Their memories living in her hands
    Would warm that sleep of mine.

Her hands remember how they played
    One time in meadow streams, –
And all the flickering song and shade
Of water took my dreams.

Swift through her haunted fingers pass
    Memories of garden things; –
I dipped my face in flowers and grass
    And sounds of hidden wings.

One time she touched the cloud that kissed
    Brown pastures bleak and far; –

I leaned my cheek into a mist
      And thought I was a star.

All this was very long ago
      And I am grown; but yet
The hand that lured my slumber so
      I never can forget.

For still when drowsiness comes on
      It seems so soft and cool,
Shaped happily beneath my cheek,
      Hollow and beautiful.
                   Anna Hempstead Branch

The child must, from the day of his birth, be
provided with whatever is conducive to his
health; and know ye this: so far as possible, the
mother's milk is best for, more agreeable and
better suited to the child, unless she should fall ill
or her milk should run entirely dry . . .
                          'Abdu'l-Bahá[1]

Unless the child, in his earliest years, be carefully
tended, whether in a material or a spiritual sense,
whether as to his physical health or his education,
it will prove extremely difficult to effect later on.
For example, if a child is not properly cared for in
the beginning of life, so that he doth not develop
a sound body and his constitution doth not

flourish as it ought, his body will remain feeble, and whatever is done afterward will take little effect. This matter of protecting the health of the child is essential, for sound health leadeth to insights and sense perceptions, and then the child, as he learneth sciences, arts, skills, and the civilities of life, will duly develop his powers . . .

'Abdu'l-Bahá[2]

When the children are ready for bed, let the mother read or sing them the Odes of the Blessed Beauty, so that from their earliest years they will be educated by these verses of guidance.

'Abdu'l-Bahá[3]

Parents should accustom themselves to treat their children, even when small, with dignity.

R. Edynbry[4]

Never speak harsh words, for once spoken they may return to you.

Dhammapada[5]

By far the most important form of attention we can give our loved ones is listening.

M. Scott Peck[6]

Let there be many windows in your soul,
>   That all the glory of the universe
>   May beautify it.

Ralph Waldo Trine

While the children are yet in their infancy feed
them from the breast of heavenly grace, foster
them in the cradle of all excellence, rear them in
the embrace of bounty. Give them the advantage
of every useful kind of knowledge. Let them
share in every new and rare and wondrous craft
and art. Bring them up to work and strive, and
accustom them to hardship. Teach them to
dedicate their lives to matters of great import,
and inspire them to undertake studies that will
benefit mankind.

'Abdu'l-Bahá[7]

Let the mothers consider that whatever
concerneth the education of children is of the
first importance. Let them put forth every effort
in this regard, for when the bough is green and
tender it will grow in whatever way ye train it.
Therefore is it incumbent upon the mothers to
rear their little ones even as a gardener tendeth his
young plants. Let them strive by day and by night
to establish within their children faith and
certitude, the fear of God, the love of the Beloved
of the worlds, and all good qualities and traits.

Whensoever a mother seeth that her child hath
done well, let her praise and applaud him and
cheer his heart; and if the slightest undesirable
trait should manifest itself, let her counsel the
child and punish him, and use means based on
reason, even a slight verbal chastisement should
this be necessary. It is not, however, permissible to
strike a child, or vilify him, for the child's
character will be totally perverted if he be
subjected to blows or verbal abuse.

'Abdu'l-Bahá[8]

O handmaids of the Merciful! Render ye thanks
unto the Ancient Beauty that ye have been raised
up and gathered together in this mightiest of
centuries, this most illumined of ages. As
befitting thanks for such a bounty, stand ye
staunch and strong in the Covenant and,
following the precepts of God and the holy Law,
suckle your children from their infancy with the
milk of a universal education, and rear them so
that from their earliest days, within their inmost
heart, their very nature, a way of life will be
firmly established that will conform to the divine
Teachings in all things.

'Abdu'l-Bahá[9]

So long as the mother faileth to train her children,
and start them on a proper way of life, the

training which they receive later on will not take its full effect. It is incumbent . . . to provide the mothers with a well-planned programme for the education of children, showing how, from infancy, the child must be watched over and taught. These instructions must be given to every mother to serve her as a guide, so that each will train and nurture her children in accordance with the Teachings.

Thus will these young plants in the garden of God's love grow and flourish under the warmth of the Sun of Truth, the gentle spring winds of Heaven, and their mother's guiding hand. Thus, in the Abhá Paradise, will each become a tree, bearing his clustered fruit, and each one, in this new and wondrous season, out of the bounties of the spring, will become possessed of all beauty and grace.

'Abdu'l-Bahá[10]

As to thy question regarding the education of children: it behoveth thee to nurture them at the breast of the love of God, and urge them onward to the things of the spirit, that they may turn their faces unto God; that their ways may conform to the rules of good conduct and their character be second to none; that they make their own all the graces and praiseworthy qualities of humankind; acquire a sound knowledge of the various branches of learning, so that from the very beginning of life they may become spiritual beings, dwellers in the Kingdom, enamoured of the sweet breaths of holiness, and may receive an education religious, spiritual, and of the Heavenly Realm. Verily will I call upon God to grant them a happy outcome in this.

'Abdu'l-Bahá[11]

The purport is this, that to train the character of humankind is one of the weightiest commandments of God, and the influence of such training is the same as that which the sun exerteth over tree and fruit. Children must be most carefully watched over, protected and trained; in such consisteth true parenthood and parental mercy.

Otherwise, the children will turn into weeds growing wild, and become the cursed, Infernal Tree, knowing not right from wrong, distinguishing not the highest of human qualities from all that is mean and vile; they will be brought up in vainglory, and will be hated of the Forgiving Lord.

Wherefore doth every child, new-risen in the garden of Heavenly love, require the utmost training and care.

'Abdu'l-Bahá[12]

Child education is a matter of the utmost importance. The infant, while yet a suckling, must receive Bahá'í training, and the loving spirit of Christ and Bahá'u'lláh must be breathed into him, that he may be reared in accord with the verities of the Gospel and the Most Holy Book.

'Abdu'l-Bahá[13]

Strive thine utmost to give his child a Bahá'í training so that when he attaineth maturity he may be merciful, illumined and heavenly.

'Abdu'l-Bahá[14]

Your responsibility as a mother, and especially as a Bahá'í mother, whose sacred obligation is to look after the training of the children along Bahá'í lines, is indeed immense. It is hoped that through God's help and guidance you will be enabled to fully discharge your duties.

Shoghi Effendi[15]

The instruction of these children is even as the work of a loving gardener who tendeth his young plants in the flowering fields of the All-Glorious. There is no doubt that it will yield the desired results; especially is this true of instruction as to Bahá'í obligations and Bahá'í conduct, for the little children must needs be made aware in their very heart and soul that 'Bahá'í' is not just a

name but a truth. Every child must be trained in
the things of the spirit, so that he may embody all
the virtues and become a source of glory to the
Cause of God. Otherwise, the mere word
'Bahá'í', if it yield no fruit, will come to nothing.

Strive then to the best of thine ability to let
these children know that a Bahá'í is one who
embodieth all the perfections, that he must shine
out like a lighted taper – not be darkness upon
darkness and yet bear the name 'Bahá'í'.

'Abdu'l-Bahá[16]

Training in morals and good conduct is far more
important than book learning. A child that is
cleanly, agreeable, of good character,
well-behaved – even though he be ignorant – is
preferable to a child that is rude, unwashed,
ill-natured, and yet becoming deeply versed in all
the sciences and arts. The reason for this is that
the child who conducts himself well, even though
he be ignorant, is of benefit to others, while an
ill-natured, ill-behaved child is corrupted and
harmful to others, even though he be learned. If,
however, the child be trained to be both learned
and good, the result is light upon light.

Children are even as a branch that is fresh and
green; they will grow up in whatever way ye train
them. Take the utmost care to give them high
ideals and goals, so that once they come of age,

they will cast their beams like brilliant candles on the world, and will not be defiled by lusts and passions in the way of animals, heedless and unaware, but instead will set their hearts on achieving everlasting honour and acquiring all the excellences of humankind.

'Abdu'l-Bahá[17]

If thou walkest in this right path, thou wouldst become a real mother to the children, both spiritually and materially. I beg of God to make thee severed from this world, attracted to the fragrances of sanctity which are being diffused from the garden of the Kingdom of El-Abhá, and a servant of the Cause of God in the vineyard of God.

'Abdu'l-Bahá[18]

Bring up a child in the way he should go.

Anon.

A rich child often sits in a poor mother's lap.

Danish Proverb

To respond to our children's needs we must change ourselves. Only when we are willing to undergo the suffering of such changing can we become the parents our children need us to be.

M. Scott Peck[19]

The greatest benefit which we have to confer on you is: Guidance to God.

When God chose us to be your parents He commanded us to offer you this guidance. Therefore, it is by His will that we give you His Holy Teaching. We speak to you of Him and of His prophets, we surround you continually with thoughts of faith and worship, and we never cease to pray for you. We cannot compel you to learn the lessons which we teach; we would not compel you if we could, for God intends our wills to be free. You must choose for yourself. Your mother and I are trying – as best we may – to follow the leading of that Guidance, and it is our hope and prayer that you will travel with us. We should be very lonely if we had to take one step without you. For this teaching which God has given us to pass on to you is the most precious thing we have to give you: more precious far than food, or clothes or schooling, or even life itself – for this knowledge is ETERNAL life.

George Townshend[20]

Ye should consider the question of goodly character as of the first importance. It is incumbent upon every father and mother to counsel their children over a long period, and

guide them unto those things which lead to
everlasting honour.

'Abdu'l-Bahá[21]

We are what we repeatedly do. Excellence, then,
is not an act, but a habit.

Aristotle

A child is as a young plant: it will grow in
whatever way you train it. If you rear it to be
truthful, and kind, and righteous, it will grow
straight, it will be fresh and tender, and will
flourish . . . girls ought to be trained in such a
manner that from day to day they will become
more self-effacing, more humble, and will defer
to and obey their parents and forebears, and be a
comfort and a solace to all.

'Abdu'l-Bahá[22]

Let us teach the ignorant, and take care of the
young child until he grows to maturity.

'Abdu'l-Bahá[23]

In relation to your specific queries, the decision
concerning the amount of time a mother may
spend in working outside the home depends on
circumstances existing within the home, which

may vary from time to time. Family consultation
will help to provide the answers.

The Universal House of Justice[24]

With regard to your question whether mothers
should work outside the home, it is helpful to
consider the matter from the perspective of the
concept of a Bahá'í family. This concept is based
on the principle that the man has primary
responsibility for the financial support of the
family, and the woman is the chief and primary
educator of the children. This by no means
implies that these functions are inflexibly fixed
and cannot be changed and adjusted to suit
particular family situations, nor does it mean
that the place of the woman is confined to the
home. Rather, while primary responsibility is
assigned, it is anticipated that fathers would play
a significant role in the education of the children
and women could also be breadwinners. As you
rightly indicated, 'Abdu'l-Bahá encouraged
women to 'participate fully and equally in the
affairs of the world'.

The Universal House of Justice[25]

With reference to the question of the training of
children: given the emphasis placed by
Bahá'u'lláh and 'Abdu'l-Bahá on the necessity for
the parents to train their children while still in

their tender age, it would seem preferable that they should receive their first training at home at the hand of their mother, rather than be sent to a nursery. Should circumstances, however, compel a Bahá'í mother to adopt the latter course there can be no objection.

Shoghi Effendi[26]

There is nothing in the teachings specifically to state that a child must not be separated from its parents and its home for the first five years of its life. In a Tablet, however, 'Abdu'l-Bahá points out that formal education at school begins when the child is five years old.

The Universal House of Justice[27]

As regards your plans: the Guardian fully approves indeed of your view that no matter how urgent and vital the requirements of the teaching work may be you should under no circumstances neglect the education of your children, as towards them you have an obligation no less sacred than towards the Cause.

Any plan or arrangement you may arrive at which would combine your twofold duties towards your family and the Cause, and would permit you to resume active work in the field of pioneer teaching, and also to take good care of your children so as to not jeopardize their future

in the Cause would meet with the whole-hearted
approval of the Guardian.

Shoghi Effendi[28]

The time and the quality of the time that their
parents devote to them indicate to children the
degree to which they are valued by their parents.

M. Scott Peck[29]

While they are at your side, love these little ones
to the utmost. Forget yourself. Serve them; care
for them; lavish all your tenderness on them.
Value your good fortune while it is with you, and
let nothing of the sweetness of their babyhood go
unprized. Not for long will you keep the
happiness that now lies within your reach. You
will not always walk in the sunshine with a little
warm, soft hand nestling in each of yours, nor
hear little feet pattering beside you, and eager
baby voices questioning and prattling of a
thousand things with ceaseless excitement. Not
always will you see that trusting face upturned to
yours, feel those little arms about your neck, and
those tender lips pressed upon your cheek, nor
will you have that tiny form to kneel beside you,
and murmur baby prayers into your ear.

Love them and win their love, and shower
on them all the treasures of your heart. Fill up

their days with happiness, and share with them
their mirth and innocent delights.

Childhood is but for a day. Ere you are
aware it will be gone with all its gifts for ever.

George Townshend[30]

When children know that they are valued, when
they truly feel valued, when they truly feel valued
in the deepest parts of themselves, then they feel
valuable. This knowledge is worth more than any
gold.

M. Scott Peck[31]

A mother understands what a child does not say.

Jewish Proverb

Mothers Educating Children

The most beautiful gift we can give each other is
the truth.

Anon.

Teach ye your children the verses that have been
divinely revealed, that they may recite them in
most melodious voices. This is what hath been set
down in His mighty Book.

Bahá'u'lláh[1]

That which is of paramount importance for the
children, that which must precede all else, is to
teach them the oneness of God and the laws of
God. For lacking this, the fear of God cannot be
inculcated, and lacking the fear of God an
infinity of odious and abominable actions will
spring up, and sentiments will be uttered that
transgress all bounds . . .

The parents must exert every effort to rear
their offspring to be religious, for should the
children not attain this greatest of adornments,
they will not obey their parents, which in a
certain sense means that they will not obey God.
Indeed, such children will show no consideration
to anyone, and will do exactly as they please.

Bahá'u'lláh[2]

It is the bounden duty of parents to rear their
children to be staunch in faith, the reason being

that a child who removeth himself from the
religion of God will not act in such a way as to
win the good pleasure of his parents and his
Lord. For every praiseworthy deed is born out of
the light of religion, and lacking this supreme
bestowal the child will not turn away from any
evil, nor will he draw nigh unto any good.

Bahá'u'lláh[3]

. . . from the very beginning, the children must
receive divine education and must continually be
reminded to remember their God. Let the love of
God pervade their inmost being, commingled
with their mother's milk.

'Abdu'l-Bahá[4]

Every child is potentially the light of the world –
and at the same time its darkness; wherefore must
the question of education be accounted as of
primary importance. From his infancy, the child
must be nursed at the breast of God's love, and
nurtured in the embrace of His knowledge, that
he may radiate light, grow in spirituality, be filled
with wisdom and learning, and take on the
characteristics of the angelic host.

'Abdu'l-Bahá[5]

Give this child a good education; make every
effort that it may have the best you can afford, so

that it may be enabled to enjoy the advantages of this glorious age. Do all you can to encourage spirituality in them.

'Abdu'l-Bahá[6]

O ye who have peace of soul! Among the divine Texts as set forth in the Most Holy Book and also in other Tablets is this: it is incumbent upon the father and mother to train their children both in good conduct and the study of books; study, that is, to the degree required, so that no child, whether girl or boy, will remain illiterate.

'Abdu'l-Bahá[7]

. . . in this new cycle, education and training are recorded in the Book of God as obligatory and not voluntary. That is, it is enjoined upon the father and mother, as a duty, to strive with all effort to train the daughter and the son, to nurse them from the breast of knowledge and to rear them in the bosom of sciences and arts. Should they neglect this matter, they shall be held responsible and worthy of reproach in the presence of the stern Lord.

'Abdu'l-Bahá[8]

It is extremely difficult to teach the individual and refine his character once puberty is passed. By then, as experience hath shown, even if every effort be exerted to modify some tendency of his, it all availeth nothing. He may, perhaps, improve somewhat today; but let a few days pass and he forgetteth, and turneth backward to his habitual condition and accustomed ways. Therefore it is in early childhood that a firm foundation must be laid. While the branch is green and tender it can easily be made straight.

Our meaning is that qualities of the spirit are the basic and divine foundation, and adorn the true essence of man; and knowledge is the cause of human progress. The beloved of God must attach great importance to this matter, and carry it forward with enthusiasm and zeal.

'Abdu'l-Bahá[9]

I pray in behalf of these children and beg confirmation and assistance for them from the Kingdom of Abhá so that each one may be trained under the shadow of the protection of God, each may become like a lighted candle in the world of humanity, a tender and growing plant in the rose garden of Abhá; that these children may be so trained and educated that they shall give life to the world of humanity; that they may receive insight; that they may bestow hearing upon the people of the world; that they may sow the seeds of eternal life and be accepted in the threshold of God; that they may become characterized with such virtues, perfections and qualities that their mothers, fathers and relatives will be thankful to God, well pleased and hopeful. This is my wish and prayer.

'Abdu'l-Bahá[10]

As to thy question concerning training children: It is incumbent upon thee to nurture them from the breast of the love of God, to urge them towards spiritual matters, to turn unto God and to acquire good manners, best characteristics and praiseworthy virtues and qualities in the world of humanity, and to study sciences with the utmost diligence; so that they may become spiritual, heavenly and attracted to the fragrances of sanctity from their childhood and be reared in a religious, spiritual and heavenly training. Verily, I beg of God to confirm them therein.

'Abdu'l-Bahá[11]

. . . the beloved of God and maid-servant of the Merciful must train their children with life and heart and teach them in the school of virtue and perfection. They must not be lax in this matter; they must not be inefficient. Truly, if a babe did not live at all it were better than to let it grow ignorant, for that innocent babe, in later life, would become afflicted with innumerable defects, responsible to and questioned by God, reproached and rejected by the people. What a sin this would be and what an omission!

Beware! Beware! that ye fail not in this matter. Endeavour with heart, with life, to train your children, especially the daughters. No excuse is acceptable in this matter.

'Abdu'l-Bahá[12]

And further, according to the Divine commandments, every child must learn reading and writing, and acquire such branches of knowledge as are useful and necessary, as well as learning an art or skill. The utmost care must be devoted to these matters; any neglect of them, any failure to act on them, is not permissible.

'Abdu'l-Bahá[13]

Bahá'í parents cannot simply adopt an attitude of non-resistance towards their children, particularly those who are unruly and violent by nature. It is not even sufficient that they should pray on their behalf. Rather they should endeavour to inculcate, gently and patiently, into their youthful minds such principles of moral conduct and initiate them into the principles and teachings of the Cause with such tactful and loving care as would enable them to become 'true sons of God' and develop into loyal and intelligent citizens of His Kingdom. This is the

high purpose which Bahá'u'lláh Himself has
clearly defined as the chief goal of every
education.

Shoghi Effendi[14]

The Guardian wishes me to assure you, in
particular, of his supplications on behalf of your
children, that they may, through Divine
confirmations and assistance, and under your
loving care and protection, receive such training
as may lead them to fully recognize and
unreservedly accept the Faith, and provide them
with the necessary spiritual equipment to
effectively and loyally serve and promote its
interests in the future.

As a Bahá'í mother you have certainly a most
sacred and weighty responsibility for their
spiritual development in the Cause, and you
should from now endeavour to instil into their
hearts the love of Bahá'u'lláh and thus prepare
them for the full recognition and acceptance of
His Station once they attain the age and capacity
to do so.

Shoghi Effendi[15]

These children must be reared with infinite,
loving care, and tenderly fostered in the embraces
of mercy, so that they may taste the spiritual
honey-sweetness of God's love; that they may

become like unto candles shedding their beams across this darksome world, and may clearly perceive what blazing crowns of glory the Most Great Name, the Ancient Beauty, hath set on the brows of His beloved, what bounties He hath bestowed on the hearts of those He holdeth dear, what a love He hath cast into the breasts of humankind, and what treasures of friendship He hath made to appear amongst all men.

'Abdu'l-Bahá[16]

. . . concern [yourself] with every means of training the girl children; with teaching the various branches of knowledge, good behaviour, a proper way of life, the cultivation of a good character, chastity and constancy, perseverance, strength, determination, firmness of purpose; with household management, the education of children, and whatever especially applieth to the needs of girls – to the end that these girls, reared in the stronghold of all perfections, and with the protection of a goodly character, will, when they themselves become mothers, bring up their children from earliest infancy to have a good character and conduct themselves well.

. . . study whatever will nurture the health of the body and its physical soundness, and how to guard their children from disease.

When matters are thus well arranged, every child will become a peerless plant in the gardens of the Abhá Paradise.

'Abdu'l-Bahá[17]

Train these children with divine exhortations. From their childhood instil in their hearts the love of God so they may manifest in their lives the fear of God and have confidence in the bestowals of God. Teach them to free themselves from human imperfections and to acquire the divine perfections latent in the heart of man. The life of man is useful if he attains the perfections of man. If he becomes the centre of the imperfections of the world of humanity, death is better than life, and nonexistence better than existence. Therefore, make ye an effort in order that these children may be rightly trained and educated and that each one of them may attain perfection in the world of humanity. Know ye the value of these children, for they are all my children.

'Abdu'l-Bahá[18]

Those children who, sheltered by the Blessed Tree, have set foot upon the world, those who are cradled in the Faith and are nurtured at the breast of grace – such must from the beginning receive spiritual training directly from their mothers. That is, the mother must continually call God to

mind and make mention of Him, and tell of His
greatness, and instil the fear of Him in
the child, and rear the child gently, in the way of
tenderness, and in extreme cleanliness. Thus
from the very beginning of life every child will be
refreshed by the gentle wafting of the love of God
and will tremble with joy at the sweet scent of
heavenly guidance. In this lieth the beginning of
the process; it is the essential basis of all the rest.

'Abdu'l-Bahá[19]

Better than a thousand useless words is the one
single word that gives peace.

Dhammapada[20]

Teaching kids to count is fine, but teaching them
what counts is best.

Bob Talbert

Educate the children in the things of God; and,
even as pearls, rear them in the heart of the shell
of divine guidance.
    Strive thou with heart and soul; see to it that
the children are raised up to embody the highest
perfections of humankind, to such a degree that
every one of them will be trained in the use of the
mind, in acquiring knowledge, in humility and
lowliness, in dignity, in ardour and love.

'Abdu'l-Bahá[21]

Pearls
lie not on the seashore.
If thou desirest one thou must
dive for it.
Oriental Tradition

And a woman who held a babe against her bosom
said, 'Speak to us of Children.' And he said:

Your children are not your children.
They are the sons and daughters of Life's
longing for itself.
They come through you but not from you,
And though they are with you, yet they belong
not to you.
You may give them your love but not your
thoughts.
For they have their own thoughts.
You may house their bodies but not their souls,
For their souls dwell in the house of tomorrow,
which you cannot visit, not even in your
dreams.
You may strive to be like them, but seek not to
make them like you.
For life goes not backward nor tarries with
yesterday.
You are the bows from which your children as
living arrows are sent forth.
The archer sees the mark upon the path of the

infinite, and He bends you with His might
that His arrows may go swift and far.
Let your bending in the archer's hand be for
gladness;
For even as he loves the arrow that flies, so He
loves also the bow that is stable.

Kahlil Gibran[22]

Mothers and Their Families

Love and respect must reign in every home. This is commended because every member of the household is a soul and as a soul he is worthy of love and respect.

Hindu Scriptures

Whatever good you expend is for parents and kinsmen, orphans, the needy, and the traveller; and whatever good you may do, God has knowledge of it.

Qur'án[1]

The family is a unit and should beseech God as one.

Qur'án

Always look up to the Highest living among your kith and kin, like the lotus that stands above its roots which are in mud.

Sikh Scriptures

If love and agreement are manifest in a single family, that family will advance, become illumined and spiritual.

'Abdu'l-Bahá[2]

According to the teachings of Bahá'u'lláh the family, being a human unit, must be educated according to the rules of sanctity. All the virtues

must be taught the family. The integrity of the
family bond must be constantly considered, and
the rights of the individual members must not be
transgressed. The rights of the son, the father, the
mother – none of them must be transgressed,
none of them must be arbitrary. Just as the son
has certain obligations to his father, the father,
likewise, has certain obligations to his son. The
mother, the sister and other members of the
household have their certain prerogatives. All
these rights and prerogatives must be conserved,
yet the unity of the family must be sustained. The
injury of one shall be considered the injury of all;
the comfort of each, the comfort of all; the
honour of one, the honour of all.

'Abdu'l-Bahá[3]

It is not so much what our parents say that
determines our world view as it is the unique
world they create for us by their behaviour.

M. Scott Peck[4]

Learning from their children is the best
opportunity most people have to assure
themselves of a meaningful old age.

M. Scott Peck[5]

If you can say that you have built genuinely loving
relationships with a spouse and children, then

you have already succeeded in accomplishing
more than most people accomplish in a lifetime.

M. Scott Peck[6]

The most important thing a father can do for his
children is to love their mother.

Rev Hesburgh

There is no greater blessing a mother can give her
daughter than a reliable sense of the veracity of
her own intuition.

Clarissa Pinkola Estés[7]

Mothers as Home-Makers

Blessed is the house that hath attained unto My tender mercy, wherein My remembrance is celebrated, and which is ennobled by the presence of My loved ones, who have proclaimed My praise, cleaved fast to the cord of My grace and been honoured by chanting My verses. Verily they are the exalted servants whom God hath extolled in the Qayyúmu'l-Asmá' and other scriptures. Verily He is the All-Hearing, the Answerer, He Who perceiveth all things.

Bahá'u'lláh[1]

The home should be a place of mutual understanding and love, of chastity and faithfulness, of reverence for the aged and respect for the young. There should be no selfishness among members of the family.

Buddhist Scriptures

The home should be a place where obedience, peace, love, generosity, humility, truth and righteous reign. Here children should respect their parents. To such a home will come contentment, knowledge, prosperity and glory.

Zoroastrian Scriptures

The highest law of the home is fidelity among its members. The wife should be faithful, the children obedient, and the father understanding and industrious. Thus will develop the perfect home.

Hindu Scriptures

Prayer should dominate the home. In it the parents and children should serve the Lord at all times. The home is a unit and it should approach the Lord as one. Here kindness to parents should govern the children and the parents should see to it that the children are nurtured rightly in all religious matters.

Qur'án

O my God! Let the outpourings of Thy bounty and blessings descend upon homes whose inmates have embraced Thy Faith, as a token of Thy grace and as a mark of loving-kindness from Thy presence. Verily unsurpassed art Thou in granting forgiveness. Should Thy bounty be withheld from anyone, how could he be reckoned among the followers of the Faith in Thy Day?

Bless me, O my God, and those who will believe in Thy signs on the appointed Day, and such as cherish my love in their hearts – a love which Thou dost instil into them.

Verily Thou art the Lord of righteousness, the Most Exalted.

The Báb[2]

I beseech God to graciously make of thy home a
centre for the diffusion of the light of divine
guidance, for the dissemination of the Words of
God and for enkindling at all times the fire of love
in the hearts of His faithful servants and
maidservants. Know thou of a certainty that
every house wherein the anthem of praise is
raised to the Realm of Glory in celebration of the
Name of God is indeed a heavenly home, and one
of the gardens of delight in the Paradise of God.

'Abdu'l-Bahá[3]

My home is the home of peace.
My home is the home of joy and delight.
My home is the home of laughter and exultation.
Whosoever enters through the portals of this
home,
    must go out with gladsome heart.
This is the home of light;
    whosoever enters here must become illumined.
This is the home of knowledge;
    the one who enters it must receive knowledge.
This is the home of love;
    those who come in must learn the lessons of
        love;
    thus may they know how to love each other.

'Abdu'l-Bahá[4]

Home-making is a highly honourable and responsible work of fundamental importance for mankind.

The Universal House of Justice[5]

As for matters of Huswifery, when God puts them upon you it would bee a sin either to refuse them or perform them negligently, and therefore the ignorance of them is a great shame and Danger for women that intend Marriage. But to seek these kinds of Businesses for pleasure, and to make them your delights, and to pride yourselves for your care and curiositie in them, is a great vanitie and Folly at best, and to neglect better things and more necessarie by pretence of being imployed is these things is surely though a common Practize, yet a peice of sinfull Hypocrisie. Doe them therefore when God puts them upon you, and doe them carefully and well, and God shall reward you, however the things themselves bee but meane, accepting them at your hands as if they were greater matters, when they are done and undergone out of Obedience to His Command. But let your Delight bee only in the better part.

Mary Ferrar

There is no such thing as a non-working mother.

Hester Mundis

Fill Thou, O God, our home with harmony and happiness, with laughter and delight, with radiant kindliness and overflowing joy, that in the union of our hearts Thy love may find a lodging place, and Thou Thyself mayst make this home of ours Thine Own!

George Townshend[6]

O God, make Thou this home of ours the garden of affection, a ripening place of love, where the hidden powers of our hearts may unfold, expand and bear the fruit of an abiding joy.

George Townshend[7]

She brings the sunshine into the house; it is now a pleasure to be there.

Cecil Beaton

Honour Thy Mother

She Walks in Beauty

She walks in beauty, like the night
      Of cloudless climes and starry skies;
And all that's best of dark and bright
      Meet in her aspect and her eyes:
Thus mellow'd to that tender light
      Which heaven to gaudy day denies.

One share the more, one ray the less,
      Had half impair'd the nameless grace
Which waves in every raven tress,
      Or softly lightens o'er her face;
Where thoughts serenely sweet express
      How pure, how dear their dwelling-place.

And on that cheek, and o'er that brow,
      So soft, so calm, yet eloquent,
The smiles that win, the tints that glow,
      But tell of days in goodness spent,
A mind at peace with all below,
      A heart whose love in innocent!

George Gordon Byron

Blessed art thou and blessed is the mother that
hath nursed thee. Appreciate the value of this
station and arise to serve His Cause in such wise

that the idle fancies and insinuations of the
doubters withhold thee not from this high resolve.

Bahá'u'lláh[1]

Blessed is the mother who bore thee and the
breast whose milk suckled thee and the bosom
wherein thou wert nurtured, because thou hast
apprehended the Day of the Lord, hast prepared
thyself to enter in unto His kingdom, hast set thy
face singly toward His Gracious Countenance,
hast believed in the Manifest Light, hast rejoiced
in the Abundant Grace, hast responded to the
Voice of thy Lord with a sincere and beating
heart and hast presented thyself from those
regions at the Glorious Threshold and hast
marked thy forehead with the pure, holy, fragrant
Tomb, the breaths of whose sanctity are spread
abroad throughout the lands as fragrant musk is
diffused unto the distant place! Then thank thy
Lord, the Merciful, the Clement, for this
great salvation and exceeding grace!

'Abdu'l-Bahá[2]

The fruits that best befit the tree of human life are
trustworthiness and godliness, truthfulness and
sincerity; but greater than all, after recognition of
the unity of God, praised and glorified be He, is
regard for the rights that are due to one's parents.

This teaching hath been mentioned in all the Books of God, and reaffirmed by the Most Exalted Pen.

Bahá'u'lláh[3]

The son shall be devoted to his father, be of the same mind with his mother . . .

Atharva Veda

Honour thy father and thy mother . . .

Exodus 20:12

For God commanded, saying, Honour thy father and mother: and, He that curseth father or mother, let him die the death. But ye say, Whosoever shall say to his father or his mother, It is a gift, by whatsoever thou mightest be profited by me; And honour not his father or his mother, he shall be free. Thus have ye made the commandment of God of none effect by your tradition.

Matthew 15:4-6.

And We have enjoined on man to be good to his parents: in travail upon travail did his mother bear him, and in years twain was his weaning:

(hear the command), 'Show gratitude to Me and to thy parents: to Me is thy final Goal.'

Qur'án[4]

Worship ye God, join with Him no peer or likeness; and show forth kindliness and charity towards your parents . . .

Qur'án

We have enjoined on man kindness to his parents: In pain did his mother bear him, and in pain did she give him birth. The carrying of the (child) to his weaning is (a period of) thirty months. At length, when he reaches the age of full strength and attains forty years, he says, 'O my Lord! Grant me that I may be grateful for Thy favour which Thou has bestowed upon me, and upon both my parents, and that I may work righteousness such as Thou mayest approve; and be gracious to me in my issue. Truly have I turned to Thee and truly do I bow (to Thee) in Islám.'

Qur'án[5]

'Say, O My people! Show honour to your parents and pay homage to them. This will cause blessings to descend upon you from the clouds of the bounty of your Lord, the Exalted, the Great . . . Beware lest ye commit that which would sadden the hearts of your fathers and mothers. Follow ye the path of Truth which indeed is a straight path. Should anyone give you a choice between the opportunity to render a service to Me and a service to them, choose ye to serve them, and let such service be a path leading you to Me. This is My exhortation and command unto thee. Observe therefore that which thy Lord, the Mighty, the Gracious, hath prescribed unto thee.

Bahá'u'lláh[6]

Be obedient and kind to thy father and mother.

'Abdu'l-Bahá[7]

Behave in such a way that your father and mother have no anxiety about you, except concerning your health.

Confucius[8]

There are also certain sacred duties of children towards parents, which duties are written in the Book of God, as belonging to God. The [children's] prosperity in this world and the kingdom depends upon the good pleasure of parents, and without this they will be in manifest loss.

'Abdu'l-Bahá[9]

If thou wouldst show kindness and consideration to thy parents so that they may feel generally pleased, this would also please Me, for parents must be highly respected and it is essential that they feel content, provided they deter thee not from gaining access to the Threshold of the Almighty, nor keep thee back from walking in the way of the Kingdom. Indeed it behoveth them to encourage and spur thee on in this direction.

'Abdu'l-Bahá[10]

. . . a father and mother endure the greatest troubles and hardships for their children; and often when the children have reached the age of maturity, the parents pass on to the other world. Rarely does it happen that a father and mother in this world see the reward of the care and trouble they have undergone for their children. Therefore, children, in return for this care and trouble, must show forth charity and beneficence, and must implore pardon and forgiveness for their parents. So you ought, in return for the love and kindness shown you by your father, to give to the poor for his sake, with greatest submission and humility implore pardon and remission of sins, and ask for the supreme mercy.

'Abdu'l-Bahá[11]

Do you realize how much you should thank God
for His blessings? If you should thank Him a
thousand times with each breath, it would not be
sufficient because God has created and trained
you. He has protected you from every affliction
and prepared every gift and bestowal. Consider
what a kind Father He is. He bestows His gift
before you ask. We were not in the world of
existence, but as soon as we were born, we found
everything prepared for our needs and comfort
without question on our part. He has given us a
kind father and compassionate mother, provided
for us two springs of salubrious milk, pure
atmosphere, refreshing water, gentle breezes and
the sun shining above our heads. In brief, He has
supplied all the necessities of life although we did
not ask for any of these great gifts. With pure
mercy and bounty He has prepared this great
table. It is a mercy which precedes asking.

'Abdu'l-Bahá[12]

O God, my God! I implore Thee by the blood of
Thy true lovers who were so enraptured by Thy
sweet utterance that they hastened unto the
Pinnacle of Glory, the site of the most glorious
martyrdom, and I beseech Thee by the mysteries
which lie enshrined in Thy knowledge and by the
pearls that are treasured in the ocean of Thy

bounty to grant forgiveness unto me and unto my
father and my mother. Of those who show forth
mercy, Thou art in truth the Most Merciful. No
God is there but Thee, the Ever-Forgiving, the
All-Bountiful.

Bahá'u'lláh[13]

It is seemly that the servant should, after each
prayer, supplicate God to bestow mercy and
forgiveness upon his parents. Thereupon God's
call will be raised: 'Thousand upon thousand of
what thou hast asked for thy parents shall be thy
recompense!' Blessed is he who remembereth his
parents when communing with God. There is,
verily, no God but Him, the Mighty, the
Well-Beloved.

The Báb[14]

Mothers' Sacrifices

There are no shortcuts to any place worth going.
Beverley Sills

Call thou to mind the behavior of Ashraf's mother, whose son laid down his life in the Land of Za (Zanján). He, most certainly, is in the seat of truth, in the presence of One Who is the Most Powerful, the Almighty.

When the infidels, so unjustly, decided to put him to death, they sent and fetched his mother, that perchance she might admonish him, and induce him to recant his faith, and follow in the footsteps of them that have repudiated the truth of God, the Lord of all worlds.

No sooner did she behold the face of her son, than she spoke to him such words as caused the hearts of the lovers of God, and beyond them those of the Concourse on high, to cry out and be sore pained with grief. Truly, thy Lord knoweth what My tongue speaketh. He Himself beareth witness to My words.

And when addressing him she said: 'My son, mine own son! Fail not to offer up thyself in the path of thy Lord. Beware that thou betray not thy faith in Him before Whose face have bowed down in adoration all who are in the heavens and all who are on the earth. Go thou straight on, O my son, and persevere in the path of the Lord, thy

God. Haste thee to attain the presence of Him
Who is the Well-Beloved of all worlds.'

On her be My blessings, and My mercy, and
My praise, and My glory. I Myself shall atone for
the loss of her son – a son who now dwelleth
within the tabernacle of My majesty and glory,
and whose face beameth with a light that
envelopeth with its radiance the Maids of Heaven
in their celestial chambers, and beyond them the
inmates of My Paradise, and the denizens of the
Cities of Holiness. Were any eye to gaze on his
face, he would exclaim: 'Lo, this is no other than
a noble angel!'

Bahá'u'lláh[1]

Lines for a Woman of Yazd

*What we have sacrificed in the path of God
no man has the right to return to us.*

(Words addressed by the mother of the young martyr 'Alí-Aṣghar
Shahíd of Yazd, to his executioners to whom she returned the
severed head of her son which they had cast
before her and his bride.)

Intent upon his devotions
or his bride's deft grace
as she bent swiftly to the samovar
he could not have imagined Carmel
half a century hence

or our complacent town, a church on every
        corner,
Shakespeare an academic rumour irrelevant
to our fathers who ran the trains,
and Islám disposed of in the locker room
by smirking seniors avid for pinups
but not yet for compassion or forgiveness.

We did not conceive of being lovable
as we applied our power to modest uses
and formulaic pieties,
drifting through conventional puerilities
into jobs, marriages and well-meant assignations,
improvising our lives from movies and pulp
        fiction,
tamping down our hunger with furtive
readings of Gibran whose diluted distillations
did not satiate the self ravenous for reality
or rid our populous dreams
of extreme and unnamed heroes.
We who reserved roses for funerals
and the graduation prom corsage
had never seen a nightingale.

How, even now, to make his swift trajection real
or voice our opsimathic wonder that one so
        young
could be so careless of corporeality?
Yet he is given us forever in his mother's words.

Sorrowing opaquely for his cruel curtailment
could she have known that
down the long dark decades
he should be needed calamitously dead
that we, adroitly trifling with illusions,
might grasp the vivid reason why we live?

What might you have chosen, mother, for your
       boy –
an obscure and virtuous longevity or
this rare and self-renewing veneration?

Take comfort, woman of Yazd.
Even in our town, now, they speak his name in
       awe.

Roger White[2]

What shall atone for the sufferings and grief of
mothers who have so tenderly cared for their
sons? What sleepless nights they have spent, and
what days of devotion and love they have given to
bring their children to maturity!

'Abdu'l-Bahá[3]

Love

In the world of existence there is no greater power than the power of Love.

'Abdu'l-Bahá[1]

One act of pure love . . . is greater than spending the whole of one's time in religious offerings to the gods, sacrificing elephants and horses.

Buddhist Scriptures

I define love thus: The will to extend one's self for the purpose of nurturing one's own or another's spiritual growth.

M. Scott Peck[2]

. . . in the world of humanity the greatest king and sovereign is love. If love were extinguished, the power of attraction dispelled, the affinity of human hearts destroyed, the phenomena of human life would disappear.

'Abdu'l-Bahá[3]

Your husband and your child have a right to your love . . .

Shoghi Effendi[4]

Your responsibility towards your son and your husband is very great, and the Guardian hopes your work will soon reach a point where you can return, at least for some time, to them, and give them that love and encouragement which is a woman's great contribution to home life.

Shoghi Effendi[5]

It is not for the love of a husband that a husband is dear; but for the love of the Soul in the husband that a husband is dear.

It is not for the love of a wife that a wife is dear; but for the love of the Soul in the wife that the wife is dear.

It is not for the love of children that children are dear; but for the love of the Soul in children that children are dear.

It is not for the love of all that all is dear; but for the love of the Soul in all that is dear.

Brihad-Aranyaka Upanishad

A mother rocks and rocks her babe to sleep in a cradle, but the thoughts of the child's sleep may so take possession of her mind that sometimes she is able to put him to sleep without the aid of the cradle. This effect is produced by the mother's magnetism.

'Abdu'l-Bahá[6]

Understand how God loves his children by
remembering the love which you bear your own
offspring.

Konkō Kyō

A loving heart is the truest wisdom.
Charles Dickens

To My Mother

Because I feel that, in the Heavens above,
  The angels, whispering to one another,
Can find, among their burning terms of love,
  None so devotional as that of 'Mother',
Therefore by that dear name I long have called
   you –
  You who are more than mother unto me,
And fill my heart of hearts, where Death installed
   you –
  In setting my Virginia's spirit free.
My mother – my own mother, who died early,
  Was but the mother of myself; but you
Are mother to the one I loved so dearly,
  And thus are dearer than the mother I
   knew
By that infinity with which my wife
  Was dearer to my soul than its soul-life.
Edgar Allan Poe

Who is it that loves me and will love me for ever with an affection which no change, no misery, no crime of mine can do away? It is you, my mother.

Thomas Carlyle, in a letter to his mother

Where there is love, nothing is too much trouble and there is always time.

'Abdu'l-Bahá

Spiritual Qualities

Of a surety, there is no greater pride and glory for a woman than to be a handmaid in God's Court of Grandeur; and the qualities that shall merit her this station are an alert and wakeful heart; a firm conviction of the unity of God, the Peerless; a heartfelt love for all His maidservants; spotless purity and chastity; obedience to and consideration for her husband; attention to the education and nurturing of her children; composure, calmness, dignity and self-possession; diligence in praising God, and worshipping Him both night and day; constancy and firmness in His holy Covenant; and the utmost ardour, enthusiasm, and attachment to His Cause.

'Abdu'l-Bahá[1]

There is the perfume of sandalwood, of rosebay, of the blue lotus and jasmine; but far above the perfume of those flowers the perfume of virtue is supreme.

Dhammapada[2]

Only the person who has faith in herself is able to be faithful to others.

Anon.

We cannot forsake self-discipline and at the same
time be disciplined in our care for another.

M. Scott Peck[3]

Let none deceive another,
Or despise any being in any state.
Let none through anger or ill-will
Wish harm upon another.
Even as a mother protects with her life
Her child, her only child,
So with a boundless heart
Should one cherish all living beings:
Radiating kindness over the entire world
Spreading upwards to the skies,
And downwards to the depths;
Outwards and unbounded . . .

Metta Sutta

Freedom from fear, purity of heart, constancy in
sacred learning and contemplation, generosity,
self-harmony, adoration, study of the scriptures,
austerity, righteousness; Non-violence, truth,
freedom from anger, renunciation, serenity,
aversion to fault-finding, sympathy for all beings,
peace from greedy cravings, gentleness, modesty,
steadiness; Energy, forgiveness, fortitude, purity, a

good will, freedom from pride – these are the
treasures of the one who is born for heaven.

Bhagavad Gita

Although the signs of material bounty are great,
yet the true bounty is that of heaven, spiritual,
which gives life eternal. Follow this and thy heart
will become as beautiful as a garden, thine eyes
bright, thy spirit happy and thy thought a
comfort to souls.

Be a well-wisher of humanity and a servant of
mankind. Thus the strength of the Kingdom will
uphold thee and the avenues of revelation open to
thee. Because today every servant is served and is
an honourable lord and every maid-servant the
queen of horizons. Grow in humility and
meekness daily, until thou attainest eternal glory
and everlasting grace.

'Abdu'l-Bahá[4]

We cannot be a source of strength unless we
nurture our own strength.

M. Scott Peck[5]

Early died
My honour'd Mother; she who was the heart
And hinge of all our learnings and our loves:
She left us destitute, and as we might

Trooping together. Little suits it me
To break upon the sabbath of her rest
With any thought that looks at others' blame,
Nor would I praise her but in perfect love.
Hence am I check'd: but I will boldly say,
In gratitude, and for the sake of truth,
Unheard by her, that she, not falsely taught,
Fetching her goodness rather from times past
Than shaping novelties from those to come,
Had no presumption, no such jealousy;
Nor by habit of her thoughts mistrust
Our Nature; but had the virtual faith that he,
Who fills the Mother's breasts with innocent
      milk,
Doth also for our nobler part provide,
Under his great correction and controul
As innocent instincts, and as innocent food.
This was her creed, and therefore she was pure
From feverish dread of error or mishap
And evil, overweeningly so call'd;
Was not puff'd up by false unnatural hopes;
Nor selfish with unnecessary cares;
Nor with impatience from the season ask'd
More than its timely produce; rather lov'd
The hours for what they are than from regards
Glanced on their promises in restless pride.
Such was she; not from faculties more strong
Than others have, but from the times, perhaps,

And spot in which she liv'd, and through a grace
Of modest meekness, simple-mindedness,
A heart that found benignity and hope,
Being itself benign.

William Wordsworth

Mothers, Bringers of Peace

War will pass when intellectual culture and activity have made possible to the female an equal share in the governance of modern national life; it will probably not pass away much sooner; its extinction will not be delayed much longer.

It is especially in the domain of war that we, the bearers of men's bodies, who supply its most valuable munition, who, not amid the clamour and ardour of battle, but, singly, and alone, with a three-in-the-morning courage, shed our blood and face death that the battle-field may have its food, a food more precious to us than our heart's blood; it is we especially, who in the domain of war, have our word to say, a word no man can say for us. It is our intention to enter into the domain of war and to labour there till in the course of generations we have extinguished it.

Olive Schreiner

Woman by nature is opposed to war; she is an advocate of peace. Children are reared and brought up by the mothers who give them the first principles of education and labour assiduously in their behalf. Consider, for instance, a mother who has tenderly reared a son for twenty years to the age of maturity. Surely she will not consent to having that son torn asunder and killed in the field of battle. Therefore, as woman advances toward the degree of man in power and privilege, with the right of vote and control in human government, most assuredly war will cease; for woman is naturally the most devoted and staunch advocate of international peace.

'Abdu'l-Bahá[1]

War and its ravages have blighted the world; the education of woman will be a mighty step toward its abolition and ending, for she will use her whole influence against war. Woman rears the child and educates the youth to maturity. She will refuse to give her sons for sacrifice upon the field of battle. In truth, she will be the greatest factor in establishing universal peace and international arbitration. Assuredly, woman will abolish warfare among mankind.

'Abdu'l-Bahá[2]

The most momentous question of this day is international peace and arbitration, and universal peace is impossible without universal suffrage. Children are educated by the women. The mother bears the troubles and anxieties of rearing the child, undergoes the ordeal of its birth and training. Therefore, it is most difficult for mothers to send to the battlefield those upon whom they have lavished such love and care. Consider a son reared and trained twenty years by a devoted mother. What sleepless nights and restless, anxious days she has spent! Having brought him through dangers and difficulties to the age of maturity, how agonizing then to sacrifice him upon the battlefield! Therefore, the mothers will not sanction war nor be satisfied with it. So it will come to pass that when women participate fully and equally in the affairs of the world, when they enter confidently and capably the great arena of laws and politics, war will cease; for woman will be the obstacle and hindrance to it. This is true and without doubt.

'Abdu'l-Bahá[3]

... when perfect equality shall be established between men and women, peace may be realized for the simple reason that womankind in general will never favour warfare. Women will not be willing to allow those whom they have so tenderly cared for to go to the battlefield. When they shall have a vote, they will oppose any cause of warfare.

'Abdu'l-Bahá[4]

... strive to show in the human world that women are ... inflexibly opposed to war and are lovers of peace. Strive that the ideal of international peace may become realized through the efforts of womankind, for man is more inclined to war than woman, and a real evidence of woman's superiority will be her service and efficiency in the establishment of universal peace.

'Abdu'l-Bahá[5]

Mothers of the New Order

The world in the past has been ruled by force, and man has dominated over woman by reason of his more forceful and aggressive qualities both of body and mind. But the balance is already shifting; force is losing its dominance, and mental alertness, intuition, and the spiritual qualities of love and service, in which woman is strong, are gaining ascendancy. Hence the new age will be an age less masculine and more permeated with the feminine ideals, or, to speak more exactly, will be an age in which the masculine and feminine elements of civilization will be more evenly balanced.

'Abdu'l-Bahá[1]

The woman has greater moral courage than the man; she has also special gifts which enable her to govern in moments of danger and crisis.

'Abdu'l-Bahá[2]

Always It is Women

It is women, always women, who reveal the way,
who see and understand what well serves life.
Forced from prehistoric day
to yield in love and birth,
to bend and stoop to cradle, fire and field
they gazed to earth

were befriended by what nurtures
and grew wise.

Men went gladly whooping to the hunt
happy with the power to devise
schemes of war, instruments of death
and magic to hold congress with the stars.
If the rich game thinned or weather turned
                    adverse
they might placate capricious spirits,
blame illest luck or totem's curse
and range afar. But women knew.
Leaning and listening they learned
what in stillness is acutely earned.
Crouched closest to the soil
they saw the berry sicken,
the water fail,
the sweet clay spoil,
knew incantation would not avail
nor sacrifice behove.
Soon the camp would move.

It was the Magdalene who as she pored
over the dust that held her Lord
read the message of the Nazarene
and knew for what the men must cast their nets.
Always it is women who reveal the way
and who, conceiving, conceive what fosters life.
But man forgets.

Again it is a woman.
At Bada<u>sh</u>t, prostrate in prayer,
she hears the shrilling trumpet pierce the air
and knows the Nightingale is listening.
Rising she tears off her veil,
steps blazing, glistening, from her tent –
the past is rent.
Men groan in consternation,
constellations pale,
the age shudders, reels and dies.

Slowly the camp moves toward
the world that she espies.

Roger White[3]

The obvious biological differences between the
sexes need not be a cause for inequality or
disunity. Rather, they are an aspect of
complementarity. If the role of women as
mothers is properly valued, their work in
nurturing and educating children will be
respected and properly rewarded. It should also
be acknowledged that the child-bearing role does
not diminish one's aptitude for leadership, or
undermine one's intellectual, scientific or creative
capacity. Indeed, it may be an enhancement.

Bahá'í International Community[4]

... with regard to spiritual education, there are
no charts, no progress reports, no quantifying
studies that can prove to the world how
important it is to equip future generations with
the virtues conducive to promoting the
establishment of unity and cooperation as the
basis for functioning in an interdependent world
community. In this respect, [we] stress the unique
advantages that educated girls bring to their roles
as mothers and first educators of the next
generation, not only as the most effective
diffusers of knowledge throughout society, but as
transmitters of core cultural and social values. It
is time that the women of the world, at least, add
a plea for education of the human spirit to the
call for educational reform.

Bahá'í International Community[5]

A commitment to educating girls is a natural
result of accepting the larger vision of society
offered by the Bahá'í teachings. Bahá'ís are
convinced that humanity is poised to achieve the
long sought harmonization of the practical and
spiritual requirements of life on earth. Far from
being at the end of evolution, humanity is really
only beginning its conscious embarkation on a
guided evolutionary pathway that will enable us
to secure the material needs for all people,
provide them with the intellectual and emotional

tools to meet life's challenges, throw off the age-old burden of warfare and militarization, and address the issues of social and economic advancement, public welfare, and the need to reverse the degradation of the environment. Clearly, a foundational component of such an enterprise is the imperative need to educate women into full partnership with men, providing them with a range of opportunities to express their newfound competencies that do not undermine their unique role as mothers – the artisans of character and the builders of civilization.

Bahá'í International Community[6]

The decision-making agencies involved would do well to consider giving first priority to the education of women and girls, since it is through educated mothers that the benefits of knowledge can be most effectively and rapidly diffused throughout society.

The Universal House of Justice[7]

The duty of women in being the first educators of mankind is clearly set forth the Writings. It is for every woman, if and when she becomes a mother, to determine how best she can discharge on the one hand her chief responsibility as a mother and on the other, to the extent possible, to participate

in other aspects of the activities of the society of
which she forms a part.

The Universal House of Justice[8]

He has created us in this radiant century, a
century longed for and expected by all the
sanctified souls in past periods. It is a blessed
century; it is a blessed day. The philosophers of
history have agreed that this century is equal to
one hundred past centuries. This is true from
every standpoint. This is the century of science,
inventions, discoveries and universal laws. This is
the century of the revelation of the mysteries of
God. This is the century of the effulgence of the
rays of the Sun of Truth. Therefore, you must
render thanks and glorification to God that you
were born in this age. Furthermore, you have
listened to the call of Bahá'u'lláh. Your nostrils
are perfumed with the breezes of the paradise of
Abhá. You have caught glimpses of the light from
the horizon of the Orient. You were asleep; you
are awakened. Your ears are attentive; your hearts
are informed. You have acquired the love of God.
You have attained to the knowledge of God. This
is the most great bestowal of God. This is the
breath of the Holy Spirit, and this consists of
faith and assurance. This eternal life is the second
birth; this is the baptism of the Holy Spirit. God
has destined this station for you all. He has

prepared this for you. You must appreciate the
value of this bounty and engage your time in
mentioning and thanking the True One. You
must live in the utmost happiness. If any trouble
or vicissitude comes into your lives, if your heart
is depressed on account of health, livelihood or
vocation, let not these things affect you. They
should not cause unhappiness, for Bahá'u'lláh
has brought you divine happiness. He has
prepared heavenly food for you; He has destined
eternal bounty for you; He has bestowed
everlasting glory upon you. Therefore, these glad
tidings should cause you to soar in the
atmosphere of joy forever and ever. Render
continual thanks unto God so that the
confirmations of God may encircle you all.

'Abdu'l-Bahá[9]

Whatever Else You Do

Whatever else you do or forbear,
impose upon yourself the task of happiness;
and now and then abandon yourself
to the joy of laughter.

And however much you condemn
the evil in the world, remember that the
world is not all evil; that somewhere
children are at play, as you yourself in the

old days; that women still find joy
in the stalwart hearts of men;

And that men, treading with restless feet
their many paths, may yet find refuge
from the storms of the world in the cheerful
house of love.

Max Ehrmann

The time of learning through suffering is coming
to an end – the time of learning through joy has
begun.

Anon.

Life's Stages

Child, child, child!
> What have they done with thee?
Where is the little child
> Who laughed upon my knee?

My son is straight and strong,
> Ready of lip and limb;
'Twas the dream of my whole life long
> To bear a son like him.

He has griefs I cannot guess.
> He has joys I cannot know:
I love him none the less;
> With a man it should be so.

But where, where, where
> Is the child so dear to me,
With the silken-golden hair,
> Who sobbed upon my knee?

Unknown

It is not yours, O mother, to complain,
Not, mother, yours to weep,
Though nevermore your son again
Shall to your bosom creep,
Though nevermore again you watch your baby
> sleep.

Though in the paler paths of earth
Mother and child, no more
We wander; and no more the birth
Of me whom once you bore,
Seems still the brave reward that once it seemed of
      yore;

Though as all passes, day and night,
The seasons and the years,
From you, O mother, this delight,
This also disappears –
Some profit yet survives of all your pangs and
      tears.

The child, the seed, the grain of corn.
The acorn on the hill,
Each for some separate end is born
In season fit, and still
Each must in strength arise to work the almighty
      will.

So from the hearth the children flee,
By that almighty hand
Austerely led; so one by sea
Goes forth, and one by land:
Nor aught of all man's sons escapes from that
      command.

* * *

And as the fervent smith of yore
Beat out the glowing blade
Nor wielded in the front of war
The weapons that he made,
But in the tower at home still plied his ringing
          trade;

So like the sword the son shall roam,
On nobler missions sent;
And as the smith remained at home,
In peaceful turret pent,
So sits the while at home the mother well content.
                                    Robert Louis Stevenson

Good-bye, my baby boy; you are gone from us for
ever!

What love did you bring with you into the
world!

What love did you stir and quicken . . .

With what love have I watched you, played
with you, tended you in all conditions, at all
hours, by day and by night; and who was happier
than I!

How many scenes made beautiful by love, and
filled with joy unroll before my eyes. Again I see
our child of longing, the first born in his first
sleep: the young adventurer voyaging from chair
to chair; the blue-clad boy among the buttercups
seeking to make playmates of the eluding

lambs . . . But all this is past. You are gone from
us, my baby-boy, and have no being now save in
the close warm embrace of your mother's
memory . . .

So must it be.

The bud perishes that the blossom may shed
its fragrance, and babyhood yields its place to the
larger life of the boy.

And have you not, my little newcomer, my
little four-year-old son, have not you all that the
baby who brought you to me had – and how
much more. What was all that baby sweetness of
yours which is now gone by save the light you cast
before you on your way to me! You too, in your
turn, will pass away from me, and the years will
ever bring to you change upon change. Deepening
happiness awaits you. You will pass from
knowledge to knowledge, from strength to
strength. And through all the years, you and I,
please God, will be the closer friends and
comrades because we have loved each other so
dearly in the baby-days gone by.

George Townshend[1]

O thou beloved maidservant of God, although
the loss of a son is indeed heart-breaking and
beyond the limits of human endurance, yet one
who knoweth and understandeth is assured that
the son hath not been lost but, rather, hath

stepped from this world into another, and she will find him in the divine realm. That reunion shall be for eternity, while in this world separation is inevitable and bringeth with it a burning grief.

Praise be unto God that thou hast faith, art turning thy face toward the everlasting Kingdom and believest in the existence of a heavenly world. Therefore be thou not disconsolate, do not languish, do not sigh, neither wail nor weep; for agitation and mourning deeply affect his soul in the divine realm.

That beloved child addresseth thee from the hidden world: 'O thou kind Mother, thank divine Providence that I have been freed from a small and gloomy cage and, like the birds of the meadows, have soared to the divine world – a world which is spacious, illumined, and ever gay and jubilant. Therefore, lament not, O Mother, and be not grieved; I am not of the lost, nor have I been obliterated and destroyed. I have shaken off the mortal form and have raised my banner in this spiritual world. Following this separation is everlasting companionship. Thou shalt find me in the heaven of the Lord, immersed in an ocean of light.'

'Abdu'l-Bahá[2]

. . . although in some ways you may be a financial burden to your children, it is to them a privilege to look after you; you are their Mother and have given them life, and through the bounty of Bahá'u'lláh they are now attracted to His Faith. Anything they do for you is small recompense for all you have done for them.

Shoghi Effendi[3]

Mother's Day

Something I have seen in the faces of old women
seamed with responses to the worst that life casts
      up
and imprinted with wry defiance
as well as resignation
speaks to me of your dreaded and unavertable
      death.
I know you will accept with regal dignity
time's last grotesqueries
but will tinge your cordial compliance with
      reluctance,
perhaps permit yourself a final *Ha!* –
no prank ever wasted on you.

You sound deceptively zestful
when my transatlantic call goes through.
Too frail now to hold the new great grandchild,

you grumble in the cheery voice you adopt for
grim announcements. *Damn old age,*
always getting in my way.

Roger White[4]

On the Receipt of My Mother's Picture

Oh that those lips had language! Life has pass'd
With me but roughly since I heard thee last.
Those lips are thine – thy own sweet smiles I see,
The same that oft in childhood solaced me;
Voice only fails, else, how distinct they say,
'Grieve not, my child, chase all thy fears away!'
The meek intelligence of those dear eyes
(Blest be the art that can immortalize,
The art that baffles Time's tyrannic claim
To quench it) here shines on me still the same
　Faithful remembrance of one so dear,
Oh welcome guest, though unexpected, here!
Who bidd'st me honour with an artless song,
Affectionate, a most lost so long,
I will obey, not willingly alone,
But gladly, as the precept were her own;
And, while that face renews my filial grief,
Fancy shall weave a charm for my relief –
Shall steep me in Elysian reverie,
A momentary dream, that thou art she.

My mother! when I learn'd that thou wast
      dead,
Say, wast thou conscious of the tears I shed?
Hover'd thy spirit o'er thy sorrowing son,
Wretch even then, life's journey just begun?
Perhaps thou gav'st me, though unfelt, a kiss;
Perhaps a tear, if souls can weep in bliss –
Ah that maternal smile! it answers – Yes.
I heard the bell toll'd on thy burial day,
I saw the hearse that bore thee slow away,
And, turning from my nurs'ry window, drew
A long, long sigh, and wept a last adieu!
But was it such? – It was. – Where art thou gone?
Adieus and farewells are a sound unknown.
May I but meet thee on that peaceful shore,
The parting sound shall pass my lips no more!
Thy maidens, griev'd themselves at my concern,
Oft gave me promise of thy quick return.
What ardently I wish'd, I long believ'd,
And, disappointed still, was still deceiv'd;
By expectation every day beguil'd,
Dupe of to-morrow even from a child.
Thus many a sad to-morrow came and went,
Till, all my stock of infant sorrow spent,
I learn'd at last submission to my lot;
But, thought I less deplor'd thee, ne'er forgot.
   Where once we dwelt my name is heard no
      more,

Children not thine have trod my nurs'ry floor;
And where the gard'ner Robin, day by day,
Drew me to school along the public way,
Delighted with my bauble coach, and wrapt
In scarlet mantle warm, and velvet capt,
'Tis now become a history little known.
That once we call'd the past'ral house our own.
Short-liv'd possession! but the record fair
That mem'ry keeps of all thy kindness there,
Still outlives many a storm that has effac'd
A thousand other themes less deeply trac'd.
Thy nightly visits to my chamber made,
That thou might'st know me safe and warmly
          laid;
Thy morning bounties ere I left my home,
The biscuit, or confectionery plum;
The fragrant waters on my cheeks bestow'd
By thy own hand, till fresh they shone and glow'd;
All this, and more endearing still than all,
Thy constant flow of love, that knew no fall,
Ne'er roughen'd by those cataracts and brakes
That humour interpos'd too often makes;
All this still legible in mem'ry's page,
And still to be so, to my latest age,
Adds joy to my duty, makes me glad to pay
Such honours to thee as my numbers may;
Perhaps a frail memorial, but sincere,
Not scorn'd in heav'n, though little notic'd here.

Could Time, his flight revers'd, restore the
            hours,
When playing with thy vesture's tissued flow'rs,
The violet, the pink, and jessamine,
I prick'd them into paper with a pin,
(And thou wast happier than myself the while,
Woulds't softly speak, and stroke my head and
            smile)
Could those few pleasant hours again appear,
Might one wish to bring them, would I wish them
            here?
I would not trust my heart – the dear delight
Seems so to be desir'd, perhaps I might.
But no – what here we call our life is such,
So little to be lov'd, and thou so much,
That I should ill requite thee to constrain
Thy unbound spirit into bonds again.

                                    William Cowper

My Texas Mother's Photograph
for Minnie Lee Bozzell

A single finger traces dust
            across the picture frame
            that holds within
            a mother's smile
            before conception came.

I stop – and trace again
feel my pain,
as muscles tense
and I cry
       for her lost youth and beauty
       now contained in glass
       as my hair greys and fades.
                    Dorothy Lee Hansen[5]

C. L. M.

In the dark womb where I began
My mother's life made me a man.
Through all the months of human birth
Her beauty fed my common earth.
I cannot see, nor breathe, nor stir,
But through the death of some of her.

Down in the darkness of the grave
She cannot see the life she gave.
For all her love, she cannot tell
Whether I use it ill or well,
Nor knock at dusty doors to find
Her beauty dusty in the mind.

If the grave's gates could be undone,
She would not know her little son,
I am so grown. If we should meet
She would pass by me in the street,

Unless my soul's face let her see
My sense of what she did for me.

What have I done to keep in mind
My debt to her and womankind?
What woman's happier life repays
Her for those months of wretched days?
For all my mouthless body leeched
Ere Birth's releasing hell was reached?

What have I done, or tried, or said
In thanks to that dead woman dead?
Men triumph over women still,
Men trample women's rights at will,
And man's lust roves the world untamed.

* * *

O grave, keep shut lest I be shamed.

John Masefield

Mother

I hoped to write to you before, but mother's dying almost stunned
my spirit . . . *Emily Dickinson*

Dear Cousins,
To value is a jeopardy,
Naught but the precious harms;
If detachment not be mastered
A loss creates alarms.

Pain's puzzling mission ratified,
Our mother slipped away
To drift into the infinite –
How brief a snowflake's day!

Persistently pain cultivates
A tenderness unknown,
Thus we lost a larger mother
Than any we had owned.

Her retreat achieved in beauty,
That solemn artist, death,
Left her portrait on the pillow –
Detail complete, save breath.

                              Emily

Roger White[6]

Mothers as a Metaphor
for Spiritual Development

Man is first born from a world of darkness, the matrix of the mother, into this physical world of light. In the dark world from whence he came he had no knowledge of the virtues of this existence. He has been liberated from a condition of darkness and brought into a new and spacious realm where there is sunlight, the stars are shining, the moon sheds its radiance, there are beautiful views, gardens of roses, fruits and all the blessings of the present world. How did he attain these blessings? Through the agency of birth from the mother. Just as man has been physically born into this world, he may be reborn from the realm and matrix of nature, for the realm of nature is a condition of animalism, darkness and defect. In this second birth he attains the world of the Kingdom.

'Abdu'l-Bahá[1]

As the babe is born into the light of this physical world, so must the physical and intellectual man be born into the light of the world of Divinity. In the matrix of the mother the unborn child was deprived and unconscious of the world of material existence, but after its birth it beheld the wonders and beauties of a new realm of life and being. In the world of the matrix it was utterly ignorant and unable to conceive of these new conditions, but after its transformation it discovers the radiant

sun, trees, flowers and an infinite range of blessings
and bounties awaiting it.

'Abdu'l-Bahá[2]

These human conditions may be likened to the
matrix of the mother from which a child is to be
born into the spacious outer world. At first the
infant finds it very difficult to reconcile itself to
its new existence. It cries as if not wishing to be
separated from its narrow abode and imagining
that life is restricted to that limited space. It is
reluctant to leave its home, but nature forces it
into this world. Having come into its new
conditions, it finds that it has passed from
darkness into a sphere of radiance; from gloomy
and restricted surroundings it has been
transferred to a spacious and delightful
environment. Its nourishment was the blood of
the mother; now it finds delicious food to enjoy.
Its new life is filled with brightness and beauty; it
looks with wonder and delight upon the
mountains, meadows and fields of green, the
rivers and fountains, the wonderful stars; it
breathes the life-quickening atmosphere; and
then it praises God for its release from the
confinement of its former condition and
attainment to the freedom of a new realm. This
analogy expresses the relation of the temporal

world to the life hereafter – the transition of the soul of man from darkness and uncertainty to the light and reality of the eternal Kingdom.

'Abdu'l-Bahá[3]

God, A Loving Mother

Thou didst create Me, O Lord, through Thy
gracious favour and didst protect Me through
Thy bounty in the darkness of the womb and
didst nourish Me, through Thy loving-kindness,
with life-giving blood. After having fashioned Me
in a most comely form, through Thy tender
providence, and having perfected My creation
through Thine excellent handiwork and breathed
Thy Spirit into My body through Thine infinite
mercy and by the revelation of Thy transcendent
unity, Thou didst cause Me to issue forth from
the world of concealment into the visible world,
naked, ignorant of all things, and powerless to
achieve aught. Thou didst then nourish Me with
refreshing milk and didst rear Me in the arms of
My parents with manifest compassion, until
Thou didst graciously acquaint Me with the
realities of Thy Revelation and apprised Me of
the straight path of Thy Faith as set forth in Thy
Book. And when I attained full maturity Thou
didst cause Me to bear allegiance unto Thine
inaccessible Remembrance, and enabled Me to
advance towards the designated station, where
Thou didst educate Me through the subtle
operations of Thy handiwork and didst nurture
Me in that land with Thy most gracious gifts.
When that which had been preordained in Thy
Book came to pass Thou didst cause Me, through
Thy kindness, to reach Thy holy precincts and

didst suffer Me, through Thy tender mercy, to dwell within the court of fellowship, until I discerned therein that which I witnessed of the clear tokens of Thy mercifulness, the compelling evidences of Thy oneness, the effulgent splendours of Thy majesty, the source of Thy supreme singleness, the heights of Thy transcendent sovereignty, the signs of Thy peerlessness, the manifestations of Thine exalted glory, the retreats of Thy sanctity, and whatsoever is inscrutable to all but Thee.

The Báb[1]

As one whom his mother comforteth, so will I comfort you.

Isaiah 40

But Chaos did not know its own creation. From its embrace with Spirit, Mōt was born. From her (Mōt, the Great Mother) it was that every seed of the creation came, the birth of all the cosmic bodies.

Philo Byblius

O God, my God! Leave me not to myself, for the extreme of adversity hath come upon me. Out of the pure milk, drawn from the breasts of Thy loving-kindness, give me to drink, for my thirst hath utterly consumed me. Beneath the shadow

of the wings of Thy mercy shelter me, for all
mine adversaries with one consent have fallen
upon me. Keep me near to the throne of Thy
majesty, face to face with the revelation of the
signs of Thy glory, for wretchedness hath
grievously touched me. With the fruits of the Tree
of Thine Eternity nourish me, for uttermost
weakness hath overtaken me. From the cups of
joy, proffered by the hands of Thy tender mercies,
feed me, for manifold sorrows have laid mighty
hold upon me. With the broidered robe of Thine
omnipotent sovereignty attire me, for poverty
hath altogether despoiled me. Lulled by the
cooing of the Dove of Thine Eternity, suffer me to
sleep, for woes at their blackest have befallen me.
Before the throne of Thy oneness, amid the blaze
of the beauty of Thy countenance, cause me to
abide, for fear and trembling have violently
crushed me. Beneath the ocean of Thy
forgiveness, faced with the restlessness of the
leviathan of glory, immerse me, for my sins have
utterly doomed me.

Bahá'u'lláh[2]

Before we were born into this world did we not
pray, 'O God! Give me a mother; give me two
fountains of bright milk; purify the air for my
breathing; grant me rest and comfort; prepare
food for my sustenance and living'? Did we not

pray potentially for these needed blessings before we were created? When we came into this world, did we not find our prayers answered? Did we not find mother, father, food, light, home and every other necessity and blessing, although we did not actually ask for them? Therefore, it is natural that God will give to us when we ask Him. His mercy is all-encircling.

'Abdu'l-Bahá[3]

. . . he who truly realizes that all women are manifestations of the Divine Mother may lead a spiritual life in the world. Without realizing God one cannot truly know what a woman is.

Sri Ramakrishna

A Mother's Prayers

I give thanks to Thee, O my God, that Thou hast suffered me to remember Thee. What else but remembrance of Thee can give delight to my soul or gladness to my heart? Communion with Thee enableth me to dispense with the remembrance of all Thy creatures, and my love for Thee empowereth me to endure the harm which my oppressors inflict upon me.

Send, therefore, unto my loved ones, O my God, what will cheer their hearts, and illumine their faces, and delight their souls. Thou knowest, O my Lord, that their joy is to behold the exaltation of Thy Cause and the glorification of Thy word. Do Thou unveil, therefore, O my God, what will gladden their eyes, and ordain for them the good of this world and of the world which is to come.

Thou art, verily, the God of power, of strength and of bounty.

Bahá'u'lláh[1]

I beseech Thee by Thy Lastness which is the same as Thy Firstness, and by Thy Revelation which is identical with Thy Concealment, to grant that they who are dear to Thee, and their children, and their kindred, may become the revealers of Thy purity amidst Thy creatures, and the manifestations of Thy sanctity amongst Thy servants.

Bahá'u'lláh[2]

My Lord! My Lord! I praise Thee and I thank Thee for that whereby Thou hast favoured Thine humble maidservant, thy slave beseeching and supplicating Thee, because Thou hast verily guided her unto Thine obvious Kingdom and caused her to hear Thine exalted Call in the contingent world and to behold Thy signs which prove the appearance of Thy victorious reign over all things.

O my Lord, I dedicate that which is in my womb unto Thee. Then cause it to be a praiseworthy child in Thy Kingdom and a fortunate one by Thy favour and Thy generosity; to develop and to grow up under the charge of Thine education. Verily, Thou art the Gracious! Verily, Thou art the Lord of Great Favour!

'Abdu'l-Bahá[3]

Praised be Thou, O Lord my God! Graciously grant that this infant be fed from the breast of Thy tender mercy and loving providence and be nourished with the fruit of Thy celestial trees. Suffer him not to be committed to the care of anyone save Thee, inasmuch as Thou, Thyself, through the potency of Thy sovereign will and power, didst create and call him into being. There is none other God but Thee, the Almighty, the All-Knowing.

Lauded art Thou, O my Best Beloved, waft over him the sweet savours of Thy transcendent bounty and the fragrances of Thy holy bestowals. Enable him then to seek shelter beneath the shadow of Thy most exalted Name, O Thou Who holdest in Thy grasp the kingdom of names and attributes. Verily, Thou art potent to do what Thou willest, and Thou art indeed the Mighty, the Exalted, the Ever-Forgiving, the Gracious, the Generous, the Merciful.

Bahá'u'lláh[4]

O Thou peerless Lord! Let this suckling babe be nursed from the breast of Thy loving-kindness, guard it within the cradle of Thy safety and protection and grant that it be reared in the arms of Thy tender affection.

'Abdu'l-Bahá[5]

O God! Rear this little babe in the bosom of Thy love, and give it milk from the breast of Thy Providence. Cultivate this fresh plant in the rose garden of Thy love and aid it to grow through the showers of Thy bounty. Make it a child of the kingdom, and lead it to Thy heavenly realm. Thou art powerful and kind, and Thou art the

Bestower, the Generous, the Lord of surpassing bounty.

'Abdu'l-Bahá[6]

O God! Educate these children. These children are the plants of Thine orchard, the flowers of Thy meadow, the roses of Thy garden. Let Thy rain fall upon them; let the Sun of Reality shine upon them with Thy love. Let Thy breeze refresh them in order that they may be trained, grow and develop, and appear in the utmost beauty. Thou art the Giver. Thou art the Compassionate.

'Abdu'l-Bahá[7]

O watchful and loving Lord! Keep our little ones this day under Thy protection. Permit no evil influence to reach or to come near them. Preserve them from illness, from accident, and from all mishap. And in the evening bring them home to their rest in safety and happiness.

George Townshend[8]

May He protect us both, May he take pleasure in us both. May we show courage together. May spiritual knowledge shine before us. May we never hate one another. May peace and peace and peace be everywhere.

The Upanishads

A Prayer for My Daughter

Once more the storm is howling, and half hid
Under this cradle-hood and coverlid
My child sleeps on. There is no obstacle
But Gregory's wood and one bare hill
Whereby the haystack and roof-levelling wind,
Bred on the Atlantic, can be stayed;
And for an hour I have walked and prayed
Because of the great gloom that is in my mind.

I have walked and prayed for this young child an
            hour
And heard the sea-wind scream upon the tower,
And under the arches of the bridge, and scream
In the elms above the flooded stream;
Imagining in excited reverie
That the future years had come,
Dancing to a frenzied drum,
Out of the murderous innocence of the sea.

May she be granted beauty and yet not
Beauty to make a stranger's eye distraught,
Or hers before a looking-glass, for such,
Being made beautiful overmuch,
Consider beauty a sufficient end,
Lose natural kindness and maybe
The heart-revealing intimacy
That chooses right, and never find a friend.

Helen being chosen found life flat and dull
And later had much trouble from a fool,
While that great Queen, that rose out of the
        spray,
Being fatherless could have her way
Yet chose a bandy-legged smith for man.
It's certain that fine women eat
A crazy salad with their meat
Whereby the Horn of Plenty is undone.

In courtesy I'd have her chiefly learned;
Hearts are not had as a gift but hearts are earned
By those that are not entirely beautiful;
Yet many, that have played the fool
For beauty's very self, has charm made wise,
And many a poor man that has roved,
Loved and thought himself beloved,
From a glad kindness cannot take his eyes.

May she become a flourishing hidden tree
That all her thoughts may like the linnet be,
And have no business but dispensing round
Their magnanimities of sound,
Nor but in merriment begin a chase,
Nor but in merriment a quarrel.
O may she live like some green laurel
Rooted in one dear perpetual place.

My mind, because the minds that I have loved,
The sort of beauty that I have approved,
Prosper but little, has dried up of late,
Yet knows that to be choked with hate
May well be of all evil chances chief.
If there's no hatred in a mind
Assault and battery of the wind
Can never tear the linnet from the leaf.

An intellectual hatred is the worst,
So let her think opinions are accursed.
Have I not seen the loveliest of woman born
Out of the mouth of Plenty's horn,
Because of her opinionated mind
Barter that horn and every good
By quiet natures understood
For an old bellows full of angry wind?

Considering that, all hatred driven hence,
The soul recovers radical innocence
And learns at last that it is self-delighting,
Self-appeasing, self-affrighting,
And that its own sweet will is Heaven's will;
She can, though every face should scowl
And every windy quarter howl
Or every bellows burst, be happy still.

And may her bridegroom bring her to a house
Where all's accustomed, ceremonious;

For arrogance and hatred are the wares
Peddled in the thoroughfares.
How but in custom and in ceremony
Are innocence and beauty born?
Ceremony's a name for the rich horn,
And custom for the spreading laurel tree.

W. B. Yeats

Night Song for a Child!

Sleep, our lord, and for thy peace
      Let thy mother's softer voice
Pray thy patrons to increase
      Freedom from all light and noise
Hark, her invocation draws
To thy guard those princely Laws!

Prince of Fire, in favour quench
      Moonlight upon wall and floor,
And with gentle shadow drench
      Candles entering at the door;
Michael, round about his bed
Be thy great protection shed.

Prince of Air, lest winds rush by
      Blustering about the park
Of this night, with watchful eye
      Keep the palings of the dark;

Raphael, round about his head
Be thy great protection shed.

Prince of Water, if thy rains
  Must to-night prevent our dearth,
Keep them from the window-panes;
  Softly let them bless the earth;
Gabriel, round about his bed
Be thy great protection shed.

Prince of Earth, beneath our tread
  And above each doubtful board
Be thy silent carpet spread;
  Let thy stillness hush our lord;
Auriel, round his bed
Be thy great protection shed.

Let your vast quaternion,
  Earth and Water, Fire and Air,
Friend him as he goes upon
  His long journey, out to where,
Princes round his final bed
Be your great protection shed.

Charles Williams

Prayers for Mothers

Thou seest, O Lord, our suppliant hands lifted up towards the heaven of Thy favour and bounty. Grant that they may be filled with the treasures of Thy munificence and bountiful favour. Forgive us, and our fathers, and our mothers, and fulfil whatsoever we have desired from the ocean of Thy grace and Divine generosity. Accept, O Beloved of our hearts, all our works in Thy path. Thou art, verily, the Most Powerful, the Most Exalted, the Incomparable, the One, the Forgiving, the Gracious.

Bahá'u'lláh[1]

Magnified be Thy name, O Lord my God! Behold Thou mine eye expectant to gaze on the wonders of Thy mercy, and mine ear longing to hearken unto Thy sweet melodies, and my heart yearning for the living waters of Thy knowledge. Thou seest Thy handmaiden, O my God, standing before the habitation of Thy mercy, and calling upon Thee by Thy name which Thou hast chosen above all other names and set up over all that are in heaven and on earth. Send down upon her the breaths of Thy mercy, that she may be carried away wholly from herself, and be drawn entirely towards the seat which, resplendent with the glory of Thy face, sheddeth afar the radiance of Thy sovereignty, and is established as Thy throne. Potent art Thou to do what Thou willest. No

God is there beside Thee, the All-Glorious, the
Most Bountiful.

Bahá'u'lláh[2]

Thine handmaid, O my Lord, hath set her hopes
on Thy grace and bounty. Grant that she may
obtain that which will draw her nigh unto Thee,
and will profit her in every world of Thine. Thou
art the Forgiving, the All-Bountiful. There is none
other God but Thee, the Ordainer, the Ancient of
Days.

Bahá'u'lláh[3]

Cast not out, I entreat Thee, O my Lord, them
that have sought Thee, and turn not away such as
have directed their steps towards Thee, and
deprive not of Thy grace all that love Thee. Thou
art He, O my Lord, Who hath called Himself the
God of Mercy, the Most Compassionate. Have
mercy, then, upon Thy handmaiden who hath
sought Thy shelter, and set her face towards
Thee.

Thou art, verily, the Ever-Forgiving, the Most
Merciful.

Bahá'u'lláh[4]

One of Thy handmaidens, O my Lord, hath
sought Thy face, and soared in the atmosphere of
Thy pleasure. Withhold not from her, O my Lord,

the things Thou didst ordain for the chosen ones among Thy handmaidens. Enable her, then, to be so attracted by Thine utterances that she will celebrate Thy praise amongst them.

Potent art Thou to do what pleaseth Thee. No God is there but Thee, the Almighty, Whose help is implored by all men.

Bahá'u'lláh[5]

Glory be to Thee, O Lord my God! I beg of Thee by Thy Name through which He Who is Thy Beauty hath been stablished upon the throne of Thy Cause, and by Thy Name through which Thou changest all things, and gatherest together all things, and callest to account all things, and rewardest all things, and preservest all things, and sustainest all things – I beg of Thee to guard this handmaiden who hath fled for refuge to Thee, and hath sought the shelter of Him in Whom Thou Thyself art manifest, and hath put her whole trust and confidence in Thee.

She is sick, O my God, and hath entered beneath the shadow of the Tree of Thy healing; afflicted, and hath fled to the City of Thy protection; diseased, and hath sought the Fountain-Head of Thy favours; sorely vexed, and hath hasted to attain the Well-Spring of Thy tranquillity; burdened with sin, and hath set her face toward the court of Thy forgiveness.

Attire her, by Thy sovereignty and Thy loving-kindness, O my God and my Beloved, with the raiment of Thy balm and Thy healing, and make her quaff of the cup of Thy mercy and Thy favours. Protect her, moreover, from every affliction and ailment, from all pain and sickness, and from whatsoever may be abhorrent unto Thee.

Thou, in truth, art immensely exalted above all else except Thyself. Thou art, verily, the Healer, the All-Sufficing, the Preserver, the Ever-Forgiving, the Most Merciful.

Bahá'u'lláh[6]

Supplicate to God, pray to Him and invoke Him at midnight and at dawn. Be humble and submissive to God and chant the verses of thanksgiving at morn and eve, for that He guided thee unto the Manifest Light and showed to thee the straight Path and destined to thee the station of nearness in His wonderful Kingdom. Verily I ask God to augment for thee, every day, the light of guidance and His gift of virtue, comfort and ease. Thus thou mayest set a good example in that region; that He may lift up the veil from before the eyes of thy mother and father, so that they may witness the lights of the Kingdom of God, which have encompassed all regions.

'Abdu'l-Bahá[7]

There is a shrine whose golden gate
Was opened by the Hand of God;
It stands serene, inviolate
Though millions have its pavement trod;
As fresh as when the first sunrise
Awoke the lark in Paradise.

'Tis compass'd with the dust and toil
Of common days, yet should there fall
A single speck, a single soil,
Upon the whiteness of its wall
The angels' tears in tears rain
Would make the temple theirs again.

Without, the world is tired and old,
But once within the enchanted door,
The mists of time are backward rolled,
And creeds and ages are no more,
But all the human-hearted meet
In one communion vast and sweet.

I enter; all is simply fair,
Not incense clouds, nor carven throne,
But in the fragrant morning air
A gentle lady sits alone;
My mother – ah! whom should I see
Within, save ever only thee?

Digby Mackworth-Dolben

Only One Mother

Hundreds of stars in the pretty sky,
    Hundreds of shells on the shore together,
Hundreds of birds that go singing by,
    Hundreds of lambs in the sunny weather.

Hundreds of dewdrops to greet the dawn,
    Hundreds of bees in the purple clover,
Hundreds of butterflies on the lawn,
    But only one mother the wide world over.

George Cooper

Bibliography

'Abdu'l-Bahá. *Paris Talks*. London: Bahá'í
Publishing Trust, 1967.

—— *The Promulgation of Universal Peace*.
Wilmette, Ill.: Bahá'í Publishing Trust, 1982.

—— *Selections from the Writings of 'Abdu'l-Bahá*.
Haifa: Bahá'í World Centre, 1978.

—— *Tablets of Abdul-Baha Abbas*. New York:
Bahá'í Publishing Committee; vol. 1, 1930; vol. 2,
1940; vol. 3, 1930.

'Abdu'l-Bahá in London. London: Bahá'í
Publishing Trust, 1982.

Arberry, Arthur J. *The Koran Interpreted*, London:
George Allen and Unwin Ltd., 1963.

The Báb. *Selections from the Writings of the Báb*. Haifa: Bahá'í World Centre, 1976.

Bahá'í International Community. *Educating Girls: An Investment in the Future*. New York, 1996.

——— *The Education of Girls: Constraints and Policy Measures*. New York, 1996.

——— *The Girl Child*. New York, 1995.

——— *Turning Point for all Nations*. New York, 1995.

Baháh'í Prayers. Wilmette, Ill.: Bahá'í Publishing Trust, 1982.

Bahá'í World, The. vol. 12. rpt. Wilmette, Ill.: Bahá'í Publishing Trust, 1980.

Bahá'í World Faith. Wilmette, Ill.: Bahá'í Publishing Trust, 2nd edn. 1976.

Bahá'u'lláh. *Gleanings from the Writings of Bahá'u'lláh*. Wilmette, Ill.: Bahá'í Publishing Trust, 1983.

——— *The Kitáb-i-Aqdas*. Haifa: Bahá'í World Centre, 1992.

——*Prayers and Meditations*. Wilmette, Ill.:
Bahá'í Publishing Trust, 1987.

Bhagavad Gita, The. Trans. Juan Mascaró.
Harmondsworth, Middx.: Penguin Books, 1962.

Compilation of Compilations, The. Prepared by
the Universal House of Justice 1963–1990. 2 vols.
[Sydney]: Bahá'í Publications Australia, 1991.

Dhammapada, The. Trans. Juan Mascaró.
Harmondsworth, Middx.: Penguin Books, 1973.

Edynbry, R. *Real Life Problems and Their Solution*.
London: Odhams Press Ltd., no date.

Esslemont, J. E. *Bahá'u'lláh and the New Era*.
London: Bahá'í Publishing Trust, 1974.

Estés, Clarissa Pinkola. *Women Who Run With the
Wolves*. New York: Ballentine Books, 1995.

Gibran, Kahlil. *The Prophet*. London: Arkana,
1992.

Hansen, Dorothy. *Cedar Berries*. Napa, CA:
Adinkra Press, 1985.

Holy Bible. King James Version. London: Collins, 1839.

Lights of Guidance: A Bahá'í Reference File. Compiled by Helen Hornby. New Delhi: Bahá'í Publishing Trust, 2nd edn. 1988.

Peck, M. Scott. *The Road Less Travelled*. London: Rider, 1983.

Qur'án, electronic version, 1997.

Rig Veda, The. Trans. Wendy O'Flaherty. Harmondsworth, Middx.: Penguin Books, 1984.

Star of the West. Rpt. Oxford: George Ronald, 1984.

Townshend, George. *The Mission of Bahá'u'lláh and Other Literary Pieces*. London: George Ronald, 1965.

Two Wings of a Bird: The Equality of Women and Men. A Statement by the National Spiritual Assembly of the United States. Wilmette, Ill.: Bahá'í Publishing Trust, 1997.

Universal House of Justice, The. *The Promise of World Peace*. Haifa: Bahá'í World Centre, 1985.

Waley, Arthur (trans.). *The Analects of Confucius*. London: Unwin Hyman, 1988.

White, Roger. *Another Song, Another Season*. Oxford: George Ronald, 1979.

—— *The Language of There*. Richmond, B. C.: New Leaf Publishing, 1992.

—— *One Bird, One Cage, One Flight: Homage to Emily Dickinson*. Happy Camp, CA: Naturegraph, 1983.

—— *Witness of Pebbles*. Oxford: George Ronald, 1981.

References

Preface
  1. From a letter written on behalf of the Universal House of Justice to an individual believer, 23 August 1984, in Lights of Guidance, p. 626.
  2. Two Wings of a Bird, p. 7.

On the Birth of a Child
  1. 'Abdu'l-Bahá, *Paris Talks*, p. 139.
  2. Al-A'Araf, 7:189.
  3. Townshend, *Mission of Bahá'u'lláh*, p. 142.
  4. ibid., p. 146

The Importance of Mothers
  1. 'Abdu'l-Bahá, *Paris Talks*, p. 162.
  2. Edynbry, *Real Life Problems*, p. 10.

The First Mentors
  1. 'Abdu'l-Bahá, *Selections*, p. 126.
  2. From a letter written on behalf of Shoghi

Effendi to an individual believer, 16 November 1939, in *Compilation*, vol. 1, pp. 303–4.
3. 'Abdu'l-Bahá, in ibid., pp. 288–9.
4. 'Abdu'l-Bahá, *Tablets*, p. 606.
5. 'Abdu'l-Bahá, *Selections*, p. 138.

Educating Mothers
1. 'Abdu'l-Bahá, *Promulgation*, p. 175.
2. 'Abdu'l-Bahá, *Tablets*, p. 580.
3. 'Abdu'l-Bahá, in *Compilation*, vol. 1, p. 368.
4. ibid. p. 284.
5. *The Girl Child*, Statement of the Bahá'í International Community.
6. ibid.
7. 'Abdu'l-Bahá, *Compilation*, vol. 1, p. 286.
8. 'Abdu'l-Bahá, *Paris Talks*, p. 162.
9. 'Abdu'l-Bahá, *Promulgation*, pp. 133–4.

Mothering
1. 'Abdu'l-Bahá, in *Compilation*, vol. 1, p. 461.
2. 'Abdu'l-Bahá, in *Lights of Guidance*, p. 294.
3. 'Abdu'l-Bahá, in *Compilation*, vol. 1, p. 280.
4. Edynbry, *Real Life Problems*, p. 15.
5. *Dhammapada*, 'Life', verse 133.
6. Peck, *Road Less Travelled*, p. 129.
7. 'Abdu'l-Bahá, *Selections*, p. 129.
8. ibid., p. 125.
9. ibid., pp. 125–6.
10. ibid., pp. 138–9.

11. 'Abdu'l-Bahá, ibid., p. 142.

12. 'Abdu'l-Bahá, in *Compilation*, vol. 1, p. 263.

13. ibid., p. 266.

14. 'Abdu'l-Bahá, *Selections*, p. 201.

15. From a letter written on behalf of Shoghi Effendi to an individual believer, 22 July 1933, in *Compilation*, vol. 1, p. 300.

16. 'Abdu'l-Bahá, *Selections*, p. 143.

17. ibid., pp. 135–6.

18. 'Abdu'l-Bahá, *Tablets*, p. 606.

19. Peck, *Road Less Travelled*, p. 149.

20. Townshend, *Mission of Bahá'u'lláh*, p. 147.

21. 'Abdu'l-Bahá, *Selections*, p. 134.

22. 'Abdu'l-Bahá, in *Compilation*, vol. 1, p. 287.

23. 'Abdu'l-Bahá, *Paris Talks*, p. 148.

24. From a letter written on behalf of the Universal House of Justice to an individual believer, 9 August 1984, in *Lights of Guidance*, p. 626.

25. From a letter written on behalf of the Universal House of Justice to an individual believer, 16 June 1982, in *Lights of Guidance*, p. 626.

26. From a letter written on behalf of Shoghi Effendi to an individual believer, 13 November 1940, in *Compilation*, vol. 2, p. 304.

27. From a letter written on behalf of the Universal House of Justice to the National Spiritual Assembly of the United States, 10 March 1975, in *Lights of Guidance*, p. 148.

28. From a letter written on behalf of Shoghi

Effendi to an individual believer, 17 July 1938, in *Compilation*, vol. 1, p. 301.

29. Peck, *Road Less Travelled*, p. 23.
30. Townshend, *Mission of Bahá'u'lláh*, p. 145.
31. Peck, *Road Less Travelled*, p. 24.

Mothers Educating Children

1. Bahá'u'lláh, in *Compilation*, vol. 1, p. 250.
2. ibid., p. 248.
3. ibid.
4. 'Abdu'l-Bahá, *Selections*, p. 127.
5. ibid., pp. 130–1.
6. *'Abdu'l-Bahá in London*, p. 111.
7. 'Abdu'l-Bahá, *Selections*, p. 127.
8. ibid., pp. 126–7.
9. ibid., p. 137.
10. 'Abdu'l-Bahá, *Promulgation*, p. 53.
11. 'Abdu'l-Bahá, *Tablets*, pp. 86–7.
12. ibid., p. 579.
13. 'Abdu'l-Bahá, in *Compilation*, vol. 1, p. 4.
14. From a letter written on behalf of Shoghi Effendi to an individual believer, 9 July 1939, in *Compilation*, vol. 1, p. 303.
15. From a letter written on behalf of Shoghi Effendi to an individual believer, 20 April 1939, in *Compilation*, vol. 1, pp. 301–2.
16. 'Abdu'l-Bahá, *Selections*, pp. 21–2.
17. ibid., p. 124.
18. 'Abdu'l-Bahá, *Promulgation*, pp. 53–4.

19. 'Abdu'l-Bahá, in *Compilation*, vol. 1, p. 280.
20. *Dhammapada*, 'Better than a Thousand', verse 100.
21. 'Abdu'l-Bahá, in *Compilation*, vol. 1, p. 272.
22. Gibran, 'Children', *The Prophet*.

Mothers and Their Families
1. Qur'án II, v. 211, p. 57.
2. 'Abdu'l-Bahá, in *Bahá'í World Faith*, p. 229.
3. 'Abdu'l-Bahá, *Promulgation*, p. 168.
4. Peck, *Road Less Travelled*, p. 189.
5. ibid., p. 150.
6. ibid., p. 159.
7. Estés, *Women Who Run With the Wolves*.

Mothers as Homemakers
1. Bahá'u'lláh, in *Compilation*, vol. 1, pp. 385–6.
2. The Báb, *Selections*, p. 200.
3. 'Abdu'l-Bahá, *Compilation*, vol. 1, p. 392.
4. *Star of the West*, vol. 9, no. 3, p. 40.
5. From a letter written on behalf of the Universal House of Justice to an individual believer, 16 June, 1982, in *Lights of Guidance*, p. 626.
6. Townshend, *Mission of Bahá'u'lláh*, p. 147.
7. ibid., p. 148.

Honour Thy Mother
1. Bahá'u'lláh, *Tablets*, p. 252.

2. 'Abdu'l-Bahá, *Tablets*, pp. 114–15.
3. Bahá'u'lláh, Kitáb-i-Aqdas, Question 106.
4. Luqman 31:14.
5. Al-Alqaf 46:15.
6. Bahá'u'lláh, in *Lights of Guidance*, pp. 229–30.
7. Source unknown.
8. Waley, *Analects*, p. 89.
9. 'Abdu'l-Bahá in *Lights of Guidance*, p. 151.
10. 'Abdu'l-Bahá, *Compilation*, vol. 1, p. 392.
11. 'Abdu'l-Bahá, *Some Answered Questions*, pp. 231–2.
12. 'Abdu'l-Bahá, *Promulgation*, pp. 187–8.
13. Bahá'u'lláh, *Tablets*, pp. 24–5.
14. The Báb, *Selections*, p. 94.

Mothers' Sacrifices

1. Bahá'u'lláh, *Gleanings*, pp. 135–6.
2. White, *Witness of Pebbles*, pp. 14–15.
3. 'Abdu'l-Bahá, *Promulgation*, p. 119.

Love

1. 'Abdu'l-Bahá, *Paris Talks*, p. 179.
2. Peck, *Road Less Travelled*, p. 81.
3. 'Abdu'l-Bahá, *Promulgation*, p. 256.
4. From a letter written on behalf of Shoghi Effendi to an individual believer, 9 March 1946, in *Compilation*, vol. 1, p. 405.
5. From a letter written on behalf of Shoghi

Effendi to an individual believer, 5 August
1946, in ibid., p. 407.
6. 'Abdu'l-Bahá, in *Lights of Guidance*, p. 517.

Spiritual Qualities
1. 'Abdu'l-Bahá, in *Compilation*, vol. 1, p. 393.
2. *Dhammapada*, 'The Flowers of Life', verse 55.
3. Peck, *Road Less Travelled*, p. 83.
4. 'Abdu'l-Bahá, *Tablets*, pp. 523–4.
5. Peck, *Road Less Travelled*, p. 83.

Mothers, Bringers of Peace
1. 'Abdu'l-Bahá, *Promulgation*, p. 375.
2. ibid., p. 108.
3. ibid., pp. 134–5.
4. ibid., p. 167.
5. ibid., p. 284.

Mothers of the New Order
1. 'Abdu'l-Bahá, quoted in Esslemont, *Bahá'u'lláh and the New Era*, p. 141.
2. *'Abdu'l-Bahá in London*, pp. 102–3.
3. White, *Another Song, Another Season*, pp. 123–4.
4. Bahá'í International Community, *Turning Point For All Nations*.
5. Bahá'í International Community, *Educating Girls: An Investment in the Future*.
6. Bahá'í International Community, *The*

Education of Girls: Constraints and Policy Measures.

7. The Universal House of Justice, *The Promise of World Peace*, p. 12.
8. From a letter written on behalf of the Universal House of Justice to an individual believer, 22 April 1981, in *Lights of Guidance*, p. 619.
9. 'Abdu'l-Bahá, *Promulgation*, pp. 188–9.

Life's Stages
1. Townshend, *Mission of Bahá'u'lláh*, p. 144.
2. 'Abdu'l-Bahá, *Selections*, p. 201.
3. From a letter written on behalf of Shoghi Effendi to an individual believer, 20 September 1948, in *Compilation*, vol. 1, p. 407.
4. White, *Language of There*, p. 50.
5. Hansen, *Cedar Berries*, p. 62.
6. White, *One Bird, One Cage, One Flight*, p. 115.

Mothers as a Metaphor for Spiritual Development
1. 'Abdu'l-Bahá, *Promulgation*, p. 332.
2. 'Abdu'l-Bahá, ibid., pp. 288–9.
3. 'Abdu'l-Bahá, ibid., p. 47.

God, a Loving Mother
1. The Báb, *Selections*, pp. 173–4.
2. Bahá'u'lláh, *Prayers and Meditations*, p. 234.
3. 'Abdu'l-Bahá, *Promulgation*, pp. 246–7.

A Mother's Prayers

1. Bahá'u'lláh, *Prayers and Meditation*, pp. 195–6.
2. ibid., p. 229.
3. 'Abdu'l-Bahá in *Bahá'í Prayers*, p. 67.
4. Bahá'u'lláh, in ibid., p. 34.
5. 'Abdu'l-Bahá, in ibid., p. 35.
6. 'Abdu'l-Bahá, in ibid., p. 35.
7. 'Abdu'l-Bahá, *Promulgation*, p. 194.
8. Townshend, *Mission of Bahá'u'lláh*, p. 135.

Prayers for Mothers

1. Bahá'u'lláh, *Gleanings*, pp. 301–2.
2. Bahá'u'lláh, *Prayers and Meditations*, pp. 147–8.
3. Bahá'u'lláh, *Gleanings*, p. 134.
4. Bahá'u'lláh, *Prayers and Meditations*, p. 148.
5. Bahá'u'lláh, ibid., p. 196.
6. Bahá'u'lláh, ibid., pp. 235–6.
7. 'Abdu'l-Bahá in *Bahá'í World Faith*, pp. 359–60.